TREATISE ON PRAYER

THE ARCHBISHOP IAKOVOS LIBRARY OF
ECCLESIASTICAL AND HISTORICAL SOURCES
Number 9
N. M. Vaporis, General Editor

TREATISE ON PRAYER

Symeon of Thessalonike

Translated by
H. L. N. Simmons

HELLENIC COLLEGE PRESS

SYMEON OF THESSALONIKE

TREATISE ON PRAYER

An Explanation of the Services
Conducted in the Orthodox Church

Translated by

H. L. N. Simmons

HELLENIC COLLEGE PRESS
Brookline, Massachusettes 02146
1984

Cover design by **Mary C. Vaporis**

Library of Congress Cataloging in Publication Data

Symeon, Archbishop of Thessalonike, 15th cent.
    Treatise on prayer.

    (Archbishop Iakovos Library of ecclesiastical and historical
sources; no. 9)
    Translation of: Peri ton hieron teleton kai theion mysterion tes
Ekklesias.
    1. Orthodoxos Ekklesia tes Hellados—Liturgy.
2. Orthodox Eastern Church—Liturgy. 3. Orthodoxos
Ekklesia tes Hellados—Doctrines. 4. Orthodox Eastern
Church—Doctrines. I. Title. II. Series.
BX350.S9213 1984   264'.0193   84-10908
ISBN 0-917653-05-X
ISBN 0-917653-06-8 (pbk.)

TABLE OF CONTENTS

General Editor's Note   ix
Preface   xi
Introduction   1

TEXT

1. PRAYER AND THE ANGELS   9
  The Jesus Prayer
2. THE SAVING NAME AND INVOCATION OF OUR LORD
  JESUS CHRIST, THE SON OF GOD, WHICH IS A HOLY
  AND DIVINELY CREATED PRAYER   13
3. OUR BLESSED FATHERS KALLISTOS AND IGNATIOS,
  WHO WROTE ON THIS HOLY PRAYER   13
4. WHAT GODLY AND OUTSTANDING THINGS THIS
  PRAYER CONTAINS   14
5. ALL CHRISTIANS—CLERICS, MONASTICS AND
  LAICS—SHOULD PRAY IN THE NAME OF THE
  LORD JESUS AT PARTICULAR TIMES   16
  The Seven Daily Services
6. THERE ARE SEVEN DAILY SERVICES APART FROM
  THE LITURGY   18
7. THE REASON FOR THE SEVEN SERVICES OF PRAISE   18
8. WHY WE BEGIN THE HYMNS TO THE SAINTS AND THE
  HOLY FESTIVALS IN THE EVENING   20
9. THE DIVINE LITURGY IS THE TASK OF THE CLERGY
  ALONE, ACCORDING TO OUR SAVIOR' AND NOT TO
  BE COUNTED AMONG THE OTHER PRAYERS   21
10. THE OBSERVANCE OF THE SO—CALLED ASMATIC
  SERVICE   21
11. THE JERUSALEM TYPIKON   22
  Midnight Office (Mesonyktion)
12. THE MIDNIGHT OFFICE AND THE SIGNIFICANCE
  OF SOUNDING THE WOODEN GONG   22

13. WHY "THROUGH THE PRAYERS OF OUR HOLY
FATHERS . . ." IS SAID AT THE BEGINNING, IF
NO PRIEST IS PRESENT   23
14. THE 50TH PSALM   24
15. THE PSALMS OF THE "BLAMELESS" (PS. 118)   24
16. WHY THE CREED IS RECITED MORNING AND EVENING
    Matins (Orthros)   24
17. THE SERVICE OF MATINS. FIRSTLY, THE SIGNIFI-
CANCE OF THE OPENING OF THE SANCTUARY
DOORS, THE ENTRANCE AND THE CENSING   26
18. THE NINE CANTICLES (ODES) WHICH ARE SUNG
IN THE KANONS   31
19. THE KATHISMATA (SESSION-HYMNS)   32
20. THE KONTAKION AND IKOS   32
21. THE EXAPOSTEILARION, THE LAUDS PSALMS
(AINOI) AND THE GREAT DOXOLOGY   33
22. THE TRISAGION HYMN   34
23. THE MEANING OF THE THRICE-HOLY: HOLY,
HOLY, HOLY, ETC.   35
24. THE EXPLANATION OF THE TRISAGION: HOLY
GOD, HOLY AND MIGHTY, HOLY AND IMMORTAL,
HAVE MERCY ON US   35
25. AGAINST PETER THE FULLER   36
26. THE TRISAGION AND A SECOND INTERPRETATION
OF THE PRAYER "OUR FATHER"   37
27. THE "GLORY BE TO THE FATHER AND THE SON
AND THE HOLY SPIRIT," AND BY WHOM IT WAS
COMPOSED   37
28. A BRIEF EXPOSITION OF THE MOST HOLY PRAYER
"OUR FATHER"   38
29. WHY WE REQUEST MERCY IN THE PRAYERS AND
BEFORE EACH SERVICE   42
30. THE SIGNIFICANCE OF "WISDOM," AND "LET US
ATTEND," AND "WISDOM, BE UPSTANDING"   43
31. THE PRAYER OF THE DISMISSAL   45
    Hours and Typika
32. FIRST HOUR (PRIME)   45
33. WHY AT EACH HOUR AND OTHER SERVICES
THERE IS A FORTY-FOLD "LORD, HAVE MERCY"   46

34. THE OTHER HOURS — THIRD, SIXTH AND NINTH —
   WITH THE FIRST HOUR 47
35. THE PSALMS OF THE THIRD, SIXTH AND NINTH
   HOURS 47
36. WE ARE WELL-ADVISED TO COMPLETE ALL THE
   SERVICES AT THREE TIMES IN HONOR OF THE
   HOLY TRINITY AND TO AVOID CARELESSNESS 49
37. THE SERVICE CALLED THE "TYPIKA" 50
38. A SHORT EXPLANATION OF THE BEATITUDES
   OF THE SAVIOR 50
39. VESPERS, THREE SERVICES BEGIN AT THE
   SANCTUARY AND END THERE: MATINS,
   THE HOLY LITURGY, AND VESPERS 51
40. THE FIRST THREE PSALMS OF THE PSALTER
   REFER PRIMARILY TO THE LORD 52
41. THE SIGNIFICANCE OF THE ENTRANCE AT
   VESPERS AND THE PRIEST'S BOWING,
   RISING AND GOING UP INTO THE SANCTUARY 58
42. WHY THE ENTRANCE IS PERFORMED MORE
   SOLEMNLY ON SATURDAY EVENINGS AND ON
   OTHER FEASTS OF OUR LORD AND THE SAINTS 59
43. THE SIGNIFICANCE OF THE ENTRANCE AT MATINS 59
44. ON SUNDAYS THE MATINS ENTRANCE IS
   PERFORMED IN THE MONASTERIES ALSO,
   AS A TYPE OF THE RESURRECTION 60
45. THE SIGNIFICANCE OF THE PROKEIMENA SUNG
   EACH DAY 60
46. THE EXTENDED LITANY AND THE PETITIONS,
   WHICH ARE MOST NECESSARY 62
47. THE LITE IN THE NARTHEX AND OTHER PROCESSIONS 63
48. THE FINAL PRAYERS OF THE LITE 65
49. WHY LIGHTS ARE ALWAYS CARRIED IN FRONT 65
50. THE SO-CALLED ARTOKLASIA (BREAKING OF BREAD) 67

Compline (Apodeipnon)

51. THE SERVICE OF COMPLINE (APODEIPNON) 68

The Cathedral Rite (Asmatic Service)

52. THE GENERAL NORMS SHOULD BE MAINTAINED 69
53. THE ORDINANCES AND PRESCRIPTIONS OF THE
   CHURCH AND THE SERVICE CALLED 'ASMATIC' 71

54. ASMATIC VESPERS   71
55. THE SIGNIFICANCE OF THE SILENT CENSING
BEFORE VESPERS AND MATINS   71
56. THE THREE "SMALL ANTIPHONS" IN ASMATIC
VESPERS   76
57. ASMATIC MATINS   79
58. THE PRAYERS RECITED IN THE NARTHEX, THE
CENSING THERE AND THE ENTRY: WHAT THESE
SIGNIFY   82
59. THE 50TH PSALM   85

The Liturgy of the Presanctified and Other Lenten Rites

60. THIRD-SIXTH HOUR (TRITHEKTE) DURING THE
FASTS AND THE LITURGY OF THE PRESANCTIFIED   88
61. WHY THE PROCESSIONAL LITANIES TAKE PLACE
OUTSIDE AND THE CROSSES AND HOLY ICONS ARE
CARRIED AROUND IN THEM   91
62. WHY THERE ARE LIGHTS AT THE PROVERBS
LECTION AT VESPERS AND THE SIGNIFICANCE OF
"THE LIGHT OF CHRIST SHINES UPON ALL"   93
63. WE MUST PROSTRATE OURSELVES COMPLETELY
AT THE ENTRANCE OF THE PRE-SANCTIFIED   94
64. THE PANNYCHIS DURING THE FIRST WEEK
OF HOLY LENT   94

The Bread of the Panagia

65. THE HOLY BREAD OF THE PANAGIA WHICH IS
ELEVATED   96
66. ORDERLINESS AT THE DINING OF MONKS
AND THE PRAYERS   98
67. THE ELEVATION OF THE BREAD OF OUR
ALL-HOLY LADY (PANAGIA)   98
Index   103

GENERAL EDITOR'S NOTE

Professor Simmons has rendered a valuable service to all those interested in prayer and in the meaning of the various services of the Orthodox Church by translating into English Saint Symeon's *Peri ton hieron teleton kai theion mysterion tes Ekklesias,* which we have entitled: *Treatise on Prayer: An Explanation of the Services of the Orthodox Church.* Orthodox Christians will be particularly interested in Saint Symeon's interpretation of the various services and prayers heard in Orthodox worship, for he gives answers to the frequently heard questions: "Why do we do this?" and "What does this mean?"

Thus, it is with great joy that I welcome Dr. Simmons' translation of Saint Symeon, archbishop of Thessalonike, as Number Nine in the "Archbishop Iakovos Library of Ecclesiastical and Historical Sources."

N. M. Vaporis
General Editor

Preface

Since I had for many years been studying the works of Symeon of Thessalonike and urging others to do the same, his canonization by the Ecumenical Patriarchate last year provided the final impetus needed for me to undertake the task of translating his religious works into English. So far as I can ascertain, this is the first translation into a modern Western European language, and I hope that this will make his works accessible to a much wider circle.

With the encouragement of the Holy Cross Orthodox Press, I have begun with the *Treatise on Prayer*, since this seems to me to provide a good introduction to the Saint's liturgiological writings and to have more general appeal than some of the others. Since the chapter divisions and headings are not from Symeon's hand, I have felt at liberty to number them consecutively 1-67, and to add some subheadings for clarity. With the scriptural references I have naturally used the numeration of the Septuagint.

My special thanks are due to Jack Shamoon and Urs Christen (Basle) and Michael and Philia Kazan (Vienna), whose generous hospitality facilitated the completion of this book considerably.

May the good saint and my readers forgive its imperfections.

H.L.N. Simmons.
Vienna, November 1982

INTRODUCTION

As David Balfour has pointed out in his admirable book on the nonreligious writings of Symeon of Thessalonike,[1] this gifted and many-sided Byzantine writer was until a few years ago much quoted but relatively little read; nobody, it seems, had even bothered to compile a complete catalogue of his surviving works, nor had any significant research been done on his biography and background. Thanks to the devoted labors of Mr. Balfour, and especially of Professor Ioannes Phountoules,[2] we are now in a much better position to assess the personality and achievments of Symeon — avoiding the one-sidedly positive or negative judgments which were common in the past.

The Life and Times of Symeon

The future saint was born in Constantinople and took the name Symeon on becoming a monk, probably out of devotion to the tenth-century hagiographer Symeon Metaphrastes, whose akolouthia he composed. It appears that he originally led a quiet life in a small kellion, possibly at the Monastery of the Xanthopouloi. However, his obvious familiarity with the rites of the Great Church of Constantinople indicates that he later spent some time at the patriarchal court. Although he himself states that he was unknown until his consecration as Archbishop of Thessalonike (probably late 1416 or early 1417), the fact that he was given such an important post shows that he was not unknown to patriarch and emperor. Similarly, the protestations of unwillingness to accept the position are a common place in ecclesiastical literature — but in fact it proved to be no bed of roses, and Symeon's health was severely undermined by the strains of his high office. It is characteristic that he attributes his preservation and recovery to the intercession of Saint Demetrios, the patron saint of Thessalonike.

1

For much of Symeon's episcopate the city was under threat from both the Venetians and the Turks and cut off from the imperial capital. Under these circumstances it was only natural that a large sector of the population should press for surrender, in order to avoid the fate of those conquered. Symeon's uncompromising loyalty to his emperor and his resolute opposition to any deals with the Venetians (on religious as well as political grounds) earned him considerable ill-feeling. History justified his stand, since the surrender of the city to the Venetians in 1423 could not prevent the final catastrophe, but merely postponed it for a few years. However, Symeon was spared the sight of his metropolis captive and his cathedral a mosque, since he died suddenly in September 1429, six months before this happened. Because of his recognized impartiality and his deep concern for the poor and afflicted, the death of Symeon was mourned by Jews and Venetians, as well as by his Orthodox flock. Although regarded as a saint by many, both among his contemporaries and by later generations, he was not formally canonized until 1981.

The Liturgiological Writings of Symeon

The surviving works of our saint reflect his extraordinarily wide range of interests and activities, and even to list all these works by title would take up too much space here.[3] Political, historical, canonistic, dogmatic, apologetic, moral, pastoral and liturgical themes were all treated by him in turn; but it was the religious writings which continued to be copied and studied by succeeding generations, and it is these which will occupy us here. For a long time the only works of Symeon available in print were those published in Migne's *Patrologia graeca* (vol. 155), which were translated into Latin, and some of them into Modern Greek, Rumanian, and Russian. The present book appears, however, to be the first version published in a modern Western European language.

The *Treatise on Prayer* forms part of a very long work, which we will refer to for the sake of brevity as the *Dialogue,*

since it is set within the loose framework of a dialogue between an archbishop and a cleric. It is made up of a number
of semi-independent treatises on dogmatic and liturgical
themes, which together form a kind of handbook for the
clergy. The first section roughly one-fifth of the whole —
consists of chapters on various heresies, especially those of
the Latins, whom Symeon obviously dislikes. The remainder
of the work is primarily concerned with liturgical matters,
dealing in turn with the following topics: general sacramental
theory; baptism, chrism and Eucharist; church buildings and
their consecration; holy orders; penance; monasticism; mar-
riage; unction; prayer and the daily services; and funeral
ceremonies. The second section of the *Dialogue* is of tremen-
dous value for the history of Byzantine Liturgy (in the wide
sense of the term) from two main aspects: 1) as a contemporary and authoritative description of how the various sacramental and worship services were performed, especially
the old Cathedral Rite (Asmatic Service); and 2) as a mysti-
cal/allegorical commentary on the whole range of liturgical
functions and objects.

In our *Treatise on Prayer*, Symeon points out with no little pride that the great church of the Thessalonians, his Cathedral of Hagia Sophia, was the last place on earth where the
ancient Greek Cathedral Rite was performed, albeit with
some modifications. Everywhere else the traditional rites
had been supplanted by the monastic-based Jerusalem
Typikon — even at the great Hagia Sophia in Constantinople.
except on three days of the year only. This irreversible process was, in fact, soon to be completed at Thessalonike also,
despite Symeon's diligent work and impassioned pleas for
the maintenance of the other tradition.

As stated above, our treatise also represents the last great
systematic mystical/allegorical exposition of liturgical matters
before the final enslavement of the Byzantine East. Being
basically a sound conservative, Symeon here, too, follows in
the foosteps of his predecessors — especially of pseudo-Dionysios the Areopagite and Maximos the Confessor — and sums
up the earlier commentaries. However, he is not afraid to

supplement earlier interpretations or even to replace them
entirely where he considers it necessary; and he is a pioneer
in extending this type of commentary in a systematic way
to virtually the whole range of persons, functions and things
associated with the sacraments and prayers of the Church.
The *Treatise on Prayer* makes up about one-fifth of the
total *Dialogue* and was later divided into sixty-seven sections
of very uneven length, which were given chapter headings.
The discourse begins with an exposition of the nature and
functions of the angels — neatly arranged in 3 x 3 groups
after the scheme of pseudo-Dionysios — and draws parallels
between the angels and mankind in their joint work of praising the Holy Trinity. This leads to a discussion of the Jesus
Prayer, which Symeon strongly recommends to all groups
in Christian society— clerics, monastics and laics.

After this general introductory section on prayer, the
"seven" daily services of praise are discussed — although the
good saint has some difficulty in squeezing the nine or ten
actual services into the framework of seven mentioned in
Psalm 118.164. One could remark that since he supports the
custom of reciting them all in three groups per day, the spec-
ific number is of secondary importance, of course. Several
chapters on general liturgical topics then introduce a detailed consideration of the individual services. Again, one could
comment that it is somewhat illogical to begin with the Midnight Office after explaining that the liturgical day begins with
Vespers; but presumably Symeon was following the lay-
out of the Greek Horologion. The order is as follows: Midnight Office; Matins; First Hour (Prime), which Symeon tries
to explain away for reasons of numerical symbolism; Third
(Terce); Sixth (Sext); Ninth (None); and the Typika; Vespers and the Artoklasia; Compline; the Asmatic Services of
Vespers and Matins; the Liturgy of the Presanctified and
other Lenten services; the Elevation of the Loaf of the Panagia and Monastic Meals. Most of his exposition should be
intelligible to a modern reader familiar with the Orthodox
services, although naturally some details have changed since
the fifteenth century.

Apart from the now vanished Cathedral Rite of Vespers

and Matins, which were obviously very impressive, we find of particular interest the combination of Trithekte (Terce-Sext) with the Liturgy of the Presanctified during periods of fasting. Perhaps this could be adapted to contemporary needs, since the point of having the Presanctified in the evening (i.e., the all-day fast) has now virtually disappeared even in our monasteries, and the usual combination of Vespers and Presanctified needs trained cantors for its proper performance. Similarly, the last chapters of the work deal with what is now an exclusively monastic rite, the Elevation of the Loaf of the Panagia. Inspired by his deep devotion to the Mother of God, Symeon ordered that this ceremony be performed at the conclusion of the Matins each day in the churches of his diocese. Perhaps this custom, too, could be adapted to contemporary parish worship.

Despite Symeon's deep reverence for the traditions of the saints and Fathers and his insistence on the maintenance of established norms and customs, he was willing to allow some modifications where these were dictated by pastoral considerations. So, for example, although he states emphatically that the Asmatic Service is senior and superior to the monastic rite, he prescribed that certain sections of the daily offices should be shortened and troparia and kanons be added (on the model of the monastic practice) in order to satisfy his flock. It should be noted that his services were still predominantly scriptural in content, since the number of poetic verses added was strictly limited, e.g., to each Ode at Matins only four on ordinary days and eight at the very most. The later proliferation of these poetic additions has reduced or even eliminated the scriptural basic structure which they were meant to enhance, and one can only hope that this imbalance will soon be corrected.[4]

However, not all of the customs supported by Symeon seem defensible today. His championing of the practice of reciting all the daily services in three clumps, for example, may make a convenient pattern for Trinitarian symbolism, but it destroys the point of having individual services as well as their own symbolism.[5]

Besides codifying and adapting the services of the Cathedral Rite for his own church — we have seen liturgical codices which he compiled for this purpose — Symeon also composed some twenty-five new prayers for the Euchologion and various akolouthiai, troparia and kanons to enrich the daily worship of his flock. All these compositions are based solidly on traditional models, as one would expect. We are fortunate that Professor Phountoules (University of Thessalonike) is editing and publishing these previously inaccessible documents, so that we should soon be in a position to make a better assessment of Byzantine worship during the last years of the Empire.

I venture to hope that the present translation of the *Treatise on Prayer* will assist in the same process — the labors involved will then be amply rewarded.

NOTES

1. D. Balfour, *The Politico-historical Works of Symeon*... (Vienna, 1979).
2. I. Phountoules, *To leitourgikon ergon tou Symeonos*... (Thessalonike, 1966).
3. For full listings and more details, see the works of Balfour and Phountoules cited above.
4. I hope to deal with this question in more detail in a separate article soon.
5. This applies even more strongly to the displacement of Matins and Vespers during Lent and especially during Holy Week, of course.

Treatise on Prayer

BY

Saint Symeon

of Thessalonike

CHAPTER 1. PRAYER AND THE ANGELS

This discourse concerning prayer is the most important, brethren, for truly this is the task entrusted to us by God, and the crown of all else. Prayer is conversation directly with God, being always with God, having one's soul united with him and one's mind inseparable, as David says: "My soul clings to you," [Ps 62.9]; and "My soul thirsts for you" [Ps 62.3]; "As the deer longs for the springs of water, so my soul longs for you, O God" [Ps 121.1]; "I will love you, O God my strength" [Ps 16.2]; and "My soul is always in your hands" [Ps 118.109]. Furthermore, he says: "I will bless the Lord at all times; his praise will always be in my mouth" [Ps 33.2]. He becomes one with the angels, unites with them in positive praise and longing: "Praise the Lord from the heavens," he says, "Praise him on high. Praise him all his angels: praise him, all you powers" [Ps 148.1]. Not that he exhorts them as though they did not praise him, but rather as having the same task and perpetual longing for God, he exhorts them and unites himself with them.

This is the reason why David, that good and angelic hymn writer, calls the whole world to the praise of God, manifesting that saving revelation and ceaseless doxology and knowledge of the Trinity which the nations have obtained through this: "Praise the Lord, all you nations: praise him, all you peoples" [Ps 116.1-2]. We are taught that there is unceasing praise of God by the angels — by Isaiah, who saw the glory of God and the angels singing the Trisagion ceaselessly, and by Ezekiel also.

9

This is primarily the task of the first orders of angels, i.e., the Seraphim and the Cherubim. The first group of these praise fervently, and so are called fiery and zealous, and these are the Seraphim. The other group excels in the depth of its knowledge and praise, and this characterizes them as Cherubim. They are many-eyed because of their excellent, ceaseless, perceptive contemplation and praise. Similarly, there are amongst us zealous holy men, fired with love and fervor and zealous prayer, as it is written: "My heart burned within me, and in my studying it will burn with fire" [Ps 38.5], and "Did not our hearts burn within us?" [Lk 24.32]. Furthermore: "Who will separate us from the love of Christ?" [Rom 8.35], and "For they persevere in prayer, made fervent by the Spirit and serving the Lord" [Rom 12.11-12]. And many among us have abundance of divine knowledge and pour forth longing for the Divine like a mighty stream: "Grace is poured upon your lips" [Ps 44.3], and "You enlarge my understanding" [Ps 118.32], and "Pour out your mercy upon us" [Ps 118.77]. Their eyes are totally fixed on God, as it is written: "My eyes are ever toward the Lord" [Ps 24.15], and "I keep the Lord always before me" [Ps 15.8]. They, being pure of heart, see the Lord.

Again, some among us also imitate the third order, the Thrones, for God dwells in them. As a throne is for rest and repose, so among them they honor God in thoughts, hymns, words, and deeds, whose repose is honor, living according to the saying: "Arise, O Lord, into your resting-place" [Ps 131.8], and "Your throne, O God, is eternal" [Ps 44.7]. In them God was pleased, and "I will dwell among them," he says, "and will walk with them" [2 Cor 6.16], and "I and the Father . . . will come to him and make our home with him" [Jn 14.23], and "Do you not know that Christ is dwelling in you unless you are inexperienced" [Rom 6.16]. This possessing of Christ, this bearing him in one's heart and mind and unceasingly remembering him, studying in him, being made fervent by desire like the Seraphim and beholding him like the Cherubim, and having him reposing in one's heart like the

Thrones, is the aim of prayer. Therefore, prayer is an excellent task for the servants of Christ above all others, for the other things are ministries and secondary. This is why David tells the other angels, who are called divine servants: "Praise the Lord, all you angels of his, mighty in strength, who carry out his commands, who hear the voice of his words." They are so fervent in zeal and in the execution of his commands, since this is a work of obedience and humility, yet — "Praise and glorify him forever," he says. In saying this he does not exhort them, but honors them because they have the same perpetual task as the other orders, and joins himself and all of us to them. This praise is offered only to God, while the other ministries of the angels occur for our benefit, since we have need of them, while God has no needs, but should be praised as benefactor because of his gracious deeds.

For this reason, after the three highest orders the other orders of angels were given names referring to ministries. Some are Virtues, and are called this because they are strengthened by God and by those orders above them, and they strengthen the lower ones. The Powers similarly are ruled by God and the first orders, and have authority over those below them. In the same way the Dominions are ruled by God and the former ones — some by nature, others by dignity and knowledge — and govern the others who are subject to them. Similarly, the third order is also intermediate, being superior to the last, since it relates to God, who creates the mighty, the authorities, and the rulers, and secondly abounds in fervor and praise.

These others again are called Principalities, as they originate and proceed from the one prime cause, the unoriginate Holy Trinity, and have authority over those below them. Others are Archangels, as they announce the divine wishes and commands, and have power over those beneath them. The last of the other orders are Angels, as they are sent for our salvation and convey the divine wishes. All these, therefore, are servants of God for those who are to inherit salvation. Moreover, they have the task of unceasing prayer, so that when in ministering to us they reveal the saving commands, they do not show themselves without hymns and prayer, but announce God to us as the cause of our being and exhort us to praise him alone. For this reason the angel who appeared to Moses said: "Put off your shoes from your feet" [Ex 3.5] in honor of God. Isaiah also heard them giving praise, as did Ezekiel and Daniel; and when Christ was born, the shepherds saw a great host of angels praising God and saying: "Glory in the highest" [Lk 2.4]. Similarly, in the Apocalypse John heard others singing, and the twenty-four Elders and those slain for the sake of the Lamb, who is the Lamb of God, the living Jesus Christ. He also heard the one who taught him the mysteries of the Apocalypse telling him: "[Do not worship me] I am your fellow-servant . . . Worship God" [Rev 22.9].

You see that all give honor to God, and with the angels they hymn him above all perpetually. This is why the preacher of the divine, Paul the angelic, seraphic one, who ascended into the third heaven, tells us: "Pray without ceasing" [1 Thes 5.17]. This he teaches not of himself, but as having received it from the Lord of All: "But watch at all times, praying". . . says the Savior [Mt 15.13], and "Watch, therefore, for you do not know when the master of the house will come" [Mt 13.35], and "Watch and pray that you may not enter into temptation [Mt 26.41]. "Stand with your loins girded and your lamps lighted, and be like men who are waiting for their master to come home from the marriage-feast, so that they may open to him immediately" [Lk 12.35-36].

Concerning inner prayer, guarding the temple and unceasing prayer, we have been taught: "Blessed is that servant whom his master will find so doing when he comes" [Mt 24.46], referring to the benefits of watchfulness and prayer, that he will set them above all creatures, showing them as gods, heavenly beings, shining brighter than the sun, that he will serve them. As it is written, "He will gird himself and seat them at table, and he will come and serve them" [Lk 12.37], i.e., he will share with them everything that he has. You see what benefits God gives to those who pray with watchfulness and penitence — may he make us worthy of these things, waking and praying always, as we have been taught.

CHAPTER 2. THE SAVING NAME AND INVOCATION OF OUR LORD JESUS CHRIST THE SON OF GOD, WHICH IS A HOLY AND DIVINELY CREATED PRAYER

There are many prayers which we will discuss in their place as far as we can. The most outstanding of all is the one given by God in the Gospels, the "Our Father," since it contains in brief all the evangelical knowledge and power. There is also the saving invocation of our Lord Jesus Christ, over which many others among our holy Fathers labored, and our golden-tongued father [St. John Chrysostom] expounded this divine prayer in three discourses, as also the God-bearing [Saint John] of the Ladder and the ascetic Nikephoros, his successor, the illuminating bishop among the saints, and the venerable Symeon the New Theologian. They and others taught worthily of the divine Spirit within them, for this prayer is said in the Holy Spirit, as Paul says: No one can say 'Jesus Christ is Lord' except by the Holy Spirit" [1 Cor 12.3] ; and all who say this are of God, as he says ". . . every spirit which confesses that Jesus Christ has come in the flesh is of God" [1 Jn 4.2].

CHAPTER 3. OUR BLESSED FATHERS PATRIARCH KALLISTOS AND IGNATIOS WHO WROTE ON THIS HOLY PRAYER

In our days in particular, our father indeed among the saints, Kallistos, the God-preaching and God-bearing and in-spired one, and his co-inspired fellow ascetic, the venerable Ignatios, being themselves of God, wrote about this holy prayer in the divine Spirit. They wrote a special book in which they philosophize spiritually, godly-minded, and loft-ily in 100 chapters — the perfect number — teaching their perfect knowledge of this matter. They were noble scions of the Queen of Cities, but rejecting all worldly things as vain, they first dwelt under obedience, virginally and monastically, while later they lived a heavenly life as ascetics, maintaining that unity in Christ which Christ himself wished for all of us. "They shone in the world like stars," as Paul says [Phil 2.15]. They achieved essentially more than most sanctified people in the way of unity and love in Christ, for they did not perceive any trace of sadness between them not even for a moment — which is almost impossible for humans to avoid. Thus, they became and are called angelic, for they guarded in themselves the peace of God, which according to Paul, is the same Jesus Christ "who has made us both one" [Eph 2.14]; "whose peace surpasses all understanding" (Phil 4.7). Having departed peacefully from this troublesome life, they now enjoy the calm of heaven and see more clearly that Jesus whom they lived with all their soul and truly sought. Now they have become one with him and share untiringly his sweet and divine light, the promise of which they had already received in the world, since they had become pure in mind and deed. They enjoyed the divine radiance which the disciples saw on the mountain and which shone in many martyrs at the hour of their martyrdom, shining like Stephan, since grace is poured out not only in their hearts, but in their faces. This is why they shone like the great Moses — as those who saw testified — shining physically like the sun. These two Fathers, having already suffered in themselves the blessed passion of divine longing and peace and experienced it in practice, clearly revealed to us in wisdom concerning the divine light and the natural energy and peace of God, calling the saints to witness, and also that concerning divine prayer.

CHAPTER 4. WHAT GODLY AND OUTSTANDING THINGS THIS HOLY PRAYER CONTAINS

This holy prayer, the invocation of our Savior: "Lord Jesus Christ, Son of God, have mercy upon me," is prayer and blessing, confession of faith and purveyor of the Holy Spirit, bringer of divine gifts and purifier of the heart, expeller of demons, indwelling of Jesus Christ, source of spiritual thoughts and godly intentions, ransomer from sin, healer of souls and bodies, conveyor of divine illumination, spring of

God's mercy and crown of revelations, and godly mysteries in
humility. In short, it is the only thing saving of itself, since it
contains the saving name of our God, Jesus Christ, the Son of
God, which is the only name we invoke, "there is no salvation for us in any other," as Paul says [Acts 4.12].

For this reason it is also a prayer, since we pray for the
divine mercy through it; a wish, since we entrust ourselves to
Christ by invoking him; a confession, because when Peter
confessed this name, he was called blessed; purveyor of the
Holy Spirit, since nobody says Jesus [is] Christ except in the
Holy Spirit [1 Cor 12.3]; bringer of divine gifts, because
Christ says of this to Peter: "I will give you the keys of the
kingdom of heaven" [Mt 16.19]; purifier of hearts, since it
beholds and names and purifies the beholder; expeller of
demons, because in the name of Jesus all demons were and
are cast out [Lk 9.48]; indwelling of Christ, since by remembering him, Christ is in us and thereby dwells in us, filling us
with joy: "I remembered God and rejoiced" [Ps 76.4]. It
is a source of spiritual thoughts and intentions, since Christ is
the treasury of all wisdom and knowledge, granting these to
those in whom he dwells. It is a ransomer from sin, because
it is said regarding this: ". . . whatever you loose on earth shall
be loosed in heaven" [Mt 16.19]; a healer of souls and bodies,
because it is written: "In the name of Jesus Christ arise and
walk" and "Aeneas, Jesus Christ heals you" [Acts 9.34];
conveyer of divine illumination, because Christ is the true
light and communicates this radiance and grace to those who
call upon him, "Let the brightness of the Lord our God be
upon us" [Ps 89.17], and "He who follows me . . . will have
the light of life" [Jn 8.12]. It is the spring of divine mercy,
since he has pity on all who call upon him and grants justice
speedily for those who cry to him. It is the crown of revelations and divine mysteries to the humble, since even to the
fisherman Peter this grace was given through the revelation of
the Father in heaven, and the apostle Paul was rapt in Christ
and heard revelations. Lastly, it is the only saving thing,
because as the apostle says, in no other way can we be saved
[Acts 4.12], and " . . . this is . . . the Savior of the World,"

the Christ [Jn 4.42]. Therefore, at the last day " . . . every tongue shall confess" and give praise, willingly and unwillingly, ". . . that Jesus Christ is Lord, to the glory of God the Father" [Phil 2.11]. This is the sign of our faith, that we are and call ourselves Christians, and witness that we are of God; for ". . . every spirit which confesses that Jesus Christ has come in the flesh is of God" and that ". . . which does not confess Jesus is not of God" [1 Jn 4.2-3], i.e. it is of the Antichrist, the Devil.

Therefore, every believer should confess this name unceasingly, both by the preaching of the faith and by the love of our Lord Jesus Christ from which nothing at all should separate us [Rom 8.35], and by the grace, forgiveness, redemption, sanctification, and illumination from his name, and above all by our salvation. In this divine name the apostles taught and worked miracles. The divine evangelist John, therefore says: "These things are written, that you may believe that Jesus is the Christ, the Son of God" (—behold the faith—) "and that believing, you might have life in his name" (—behold the salvation and the life) [Jn 20.31].

CHAPTER 5. ALL CHRISTIANS — CLERGY, MONASTICS AND LAITY — SHOULD PRAY IN THE NAME OF JESUS CHRIST AT PARTICULAR TIMES

Therefore, every pious person ought always to say this name as a prayer, both with his mind and with his tongue, whether sitting or walking, and to strive always to this end. He will find great calm and joy, as all who have concerned themselves with this did in practice. Since this is a work loftier than those found even in the lives of the monks, those who are in the midst of the turmoil of the world should do this at particular times, having this as their task and performing this prayer to the best of their ability, whether clergy, monastics or laity.

The monastics should do it because they are set apart for this and have an indispensable duty to perform it, even amidst the bustle of ministration and distraction; and to pray unceasingly to God, even despite confusion, distraction, and the so-called "captivity of the mind." They should not neglect it, deceived by the Enemy, but should return repeatedly to prayer and do so rejoicing. The clergy should do it with care as an apostolic task, as divine preaching, as a work which participates in divine energies and commends us to the love of Christ. The laity similarly, so that they receive the seal and sign of the faith, as protection, sanctification, and dispeller of all temptation.

So then, all of us — clergy, monastics, and laity — should think of the Lord first, as soon as we rise from sleep, calling Christ to mind and offering this prayer as a commemoration, as first fruits and sacrifice to him, before every other concern. For before all things we should remember Christ, who saved us and loved us so much, since we are Christians, having put on Christ in baptism and having been sealed with myron, having partaken and continuing to partake of his holy body and blood, and being his members and temple, since he dwells in us. So we need to love him and carry his memory with us in our hearts. As far as possible, then, let everybody have a particular time for this prayer as an unavoidable duty.

Enough has been said about this, since those who wish can find many dealing with this teaching. Let us now begin to discuss the divine prayers of the Church according to our promise — how they are performed in order, and what is to be said about them.

Firstly, we say that the work of prayer belongs to the angels, as we stated above, and is, therefore, the special concern of the Church. Every other work, i.e., charity, nursing the brethren, visiting the sick, caring for prisoners, releasing captives, and other similar things, is done by the brethren in love and offered by them to God. Similarly, poverty, fasting, sleeping on the ground, prostrations, vigils, etc. are good and like a sacrifice to God, because they aim to subdue and humble the body so that we may be purified and approach God and become friends of God — yet these things do not present us directly to God, whereas prayer does so and unites us with him. A person praying acts towards God like a friend — conversing, confiding, requesting — and through this becomes one with our Maker himself.

Prayer should be unceasing and tireless, as it is with the angels, since this is all that God asks of us: that we keep his memory always in our souls, that we should be with him and seek him only, to love him and behold him clearly and directly. However, since this unceasing prayer is impossible because of our veil of flesh and bodily needs, and is granted only rarely to very few "equal-to-the-angels" as a gift of God, the Church has, therefore, of necessity, set certain times for prayer, at which times it is indispensable that all the faithful should pray.

CHAPTER 6. THERE ARE SEVEN DAILY SERVICES APART FROM THE LITURGY

The times of prayer and the services are seven in number, like the number of gifts of the Spirit, since the holy prayers are from the Spirit. They are as follows: Midnight Office, Matins joined with the First Hour (Prime), the Third, the Sixth and the Ninth, Vespers and Compline. The prophet David refers to them: "Seven times a day have I praised you" [Ps 118.164]. And he mentions each hour of prayer: "At midnight I arose" [Ps 118.62]; "My God, my God, for you I arise early" [Ps 62.2]; "In the morning let him hear my voice: I will come before you, and you will regard me" [Ps 5.4]. Regarding the Third, Sixth and Vespers, he says. "In the evening, in the morning and at noon I will speak and call, and he will hear my voice" [Ps 54.48]; and regarding Compline, "Every night I will water my couch, I will wash my bed with my tears" [Ps 6.7].

CHAPTER 7. THE REASON FOR THE SEVEN SERVICES OF PRAISE

The reason for each service is as follows: the *Midnight Office,* because of the unsleeping and ceaseless praise of the angels, and the calm and peace of the mind during the divine doxology, and the Resurrection — for the Lord arose early on the sabbath. Also, because of his second coming, which all of us faithful look for, when he will raise us from death as from sleep. For he is the bridegroom of souls, as it is said: He will come in the middle of the night, and we must be watchful. *Matins,* to praise the author of light at the coming of the day, the dissolver of the darkness of error and the granter of the light of piety. This is why the praise of the First Hour is joined onto Matins, as being the first fruits of the day, offering a gift and a sacrifice of praise to God, who reveals himself through the light illuminating all his creatures. Therefore, with the angels we call upon God in praise. We pray the *Third Hour* in honor of the Trinity, because a quarter of the day (an arrangement composed of four elements) has passed and because of the indwelling of the Holy Spirit at the third hour. Similarly, the *Sixth,* to the glory of the Trinity which brought forth everything and because the space of three hours (another quarter of the four-part order of the day) is past, and is the very middle of the day. At this hour, also the Sixth, he who became incarnate for us was crucified on our behalf. And the praise of the *Ninth* in honor of the Trinity, because three hours have passed since the Sixth. Similarly *Vespers* at the twelfth hour, since three hours have passed since the Ninth Hour.

The praise of the *Third Hour* especially, as we have said, for the Holy Trinity, the God of all and our only God, since at this hour the judgment against the Savior was given, and at this hour the Holy Spirit descended on the Apostles, through whom all of us faithful in the world have been illuminated.

The thanksgiving of the *Sixth* Hour being the middle of the day, and because darkness occurred in the whole land when the Savior suffered in the flesh for us.

The praise of the *Ninth Hour,* as coming towards the end of the day, and since nine testifies to the Trinity thrice; and especially since at this hour the Savior cried out and gave up his divine soul to the Father, the perfect sacrifice taking place for us, he being offered in body and soul to our God and Father on behalf of all. Then also the earth shook and the rocks split, and the graves opened as a prelude to the general resurrection, many bodies of the departed saints arose, since by the death of the Lord death was put to death and those in

Hades were freed. Through his holy soul commended to the
Father, and his flesh given voluntarily for the sacrifice of the
Cross, our souls are saved from the hands of the devil, and
our bodies granted immortality because he has risen. Therefore, let us thank him who died in the flesh for us, commended our souls into the hands of the Father through his
holy soul, and by his death, brought us to life again.

The praise of *Vespers* testifies to the following: we praise
our creator, since we have come to the end of the day, and
dedicated all of it to God. We give thanks for these things
also: for our life and nourishment, for thoughts and words
and deeds; we petition that we may pass the night in peace,
without sin or scandal, for this is a prelude to the end of our
lives when the night of death comes to us.

CHAPTER 8. WHY WE BEGIN THE HYMNS TO THE SAINTS AND THE HOLY FESTIVALS IN THE EVENING

The reason why we begin the commemoration of the
saints from the hymns of Vespers is that they lived in the day
and the light of the grace of God; and having finished the day
of this life, they are in the spirit in the unsetting light, while
in the body they are still held by death, awaiting the final
unending day when, as bearers of the promise, they will arise
with us and be made perfect with us there in the flesh.

Compline is thanksgiving for the night, by which we receive rest from our toil and a reminder of death, which will
subsequently come to us, as the first fruits of night. It, too, is
a gift of God, and one of the things made by him for us and
the rest of creation. May we pass through it unscathed by
the harmful, destructive, dark, and sinister demons — Christ
our God save us from them!

This is the order of the hymns, the seven services of
praise mentioned by David. This harmony and order takes
place, as written in the Typikon of the Church. There are two
kinds of typikon — one is that of the catholic Church, and
one which sets out only how the order of the Holy Liturgy
is to be observed.

CHAPTER 9. THE DIVINE LITURGY IS THE TASK OF THE CLERGY ALONE, ACCORDING TO OUR SAVIOR, AND NOT TO BE COUNTED AMONG THE OTHER PRAYERS

This divine and most holy service of services is not one of the seven services of praise, but separate and from Jesus alone, and the task of the clergy. This is why we did not mention it among the doxologies, since it is not counted with them. It is something special, the work of God alone, performed by his priests and not by anybody else.

The other services are at present not performed according to the Typikon of the Great Church by the other churches, nor even in the Christ-loving and royal City, since it was captured by the Latins and the tradition of its good and ancient customs destroyed. I know that it requires many priests and cantors, but the Asmatic Service is performed on the feast of the Exaltation, and at the Dormition of the Mother of God and the commemoration of Saint John Chrysostom. However, the prayers of Vespers and Matins (also called the Dawn Prayers) still witness to this, having been preserved according to the old pattern, as also those for the service called Pannychis, for the Vespers Prayers are from this service. The priestly prayers to God mention the things which the singers are chanting. The prayer of the 50th Psalm also witnesses to this, as does that of the Psalms (Lauds). However, this Asmatic Service has been abandoned in other cities, although it is well constructed of psalms and refrains offered to God. Only in this our most godly city of Thessalonike, does its Great Church preserve and maintain it — as you can see, brother — in accordance with the laudable and ancient customs of those Great Churches, i.e., of our capital, of Antioch, and of many others.

CHAPTER 10. THE OBSERVANCE OF THE SO-CALLED ASMATIC SERVICE

I beseech you in Christ that this order be maintained forever, and that the tradition of the Fathers remain among you as a kind of divine spark. We wish this to be observed and maintained always, because as sweetening and seasoning we have added kanons to it, lest some person make claims without knowledge of the order, being lukewarm and slothful and finding excuses for moving to abolish it, on the pretext that we do not hear the usual kanons which everyone sings. So these have now been added, and for the careful and zealous it has become better and pleasanter than the services celebrated in the monasteries.

CHAPTER 11. THE JERUSALEM TYPIKON

In the monasteries here, and in almost all of the churches, the order followed is that of the Jerusalem Typikon of Saint Sabas. For this can be performed by one person, having been compiled by monks, and is often celebrated without chants in the cenobitic monasteries. Such a rite is necessary and patristic, since our holy Father Savas set this down, having received it from our Fathers among the saints Euthymios and Theoktistos, and they had received it from their predecessors, including the confessor Chariton.

This order of Saint Sabas was lost, as we know, when the place was destroyed by barbarians, but was formulated by our father among the saints Sophronios, patriarch of the Holy City, and after him our holy and theological father, John Damascene, renewed it and handed it down in writing. All the holy monasteries and churches follow this order, except certain ones specially authorized from time to time by the Great Church of Constantinople according to ancient custom, and similarly in other secular churches, since they cannot observe all that is laid down. They do not read the Psalter except during the Great and Holy Lent, while the other holy monasteries follow this order.

CHAPTER 12. THE MIDNIGHT OFFICE, AND THE SIGNIFICANCE OF SOUNDING THE WOODEN GONG

At midnight or a little later, when the wooden gong has

been sounded as typifying the last trumpet of the angel, all rise from sleep as from death. In the narthex before the church, as on earth before heaven, the priest gives the blessing, typifying Christ whose priesthood adorns him. The priest must begin the prayers, and he and all of us must begin with God. Then the brothers all say together: "Glory to you, our God, glory to you," adding the usual things; for first one must offer praise to God, and then recite the rest.

CHAPTER 13. WHY "THROUGH THE PRAYERS OF OUR HOLY FATHERS . . . " IS SAID AT THE BEGINNING, IF NO PRIEST IS PRESENT

If there is no priest, the first of the brothers — or one of them — begins, but does not give the blessing, since he does not have this grace. Instead he calls on Christ to have mercy through the prayers of the Fathers, humbling himself in Christ and not trusting in himself but in the prayers of the Fathers he invokes. Among them are bishops and priests, but also the whole choir of saints who are called Fathers. Then they call upon the Holy Spirit who makes prayers perfect, to come and dwell in us, to cleanse and save us. For we do not know how to pray as we should, unless we are guided by the Holy Spirit: "For we live in him and pray through him," Paul says, "and in him we cry Abba, Father" [Rom 8.15]. Then, in imitation of the angels, they recite the Trisagion, "Most-holy Trinity," for the mercy of the Holy Trinity and as praise similar to that of the angels, and confession of the one God in Trinity.

Then they add the God-given prayer which we will expound in another place, although many have interpreted the divine wisdom relating to this, especially Gregory of Nyssa. Finally, when the priest has recited the prayer as doxology, "Lord, have mercy" is said twelve times — for the twelve-hour periods of the night and day. Then they say: "Come let us fall down . . ." three times, as David sang and as Athanasios the Great recommended be said as an introduction to the services; for he alone is our king and our eternal Christ, with the

Father and the Holy Spirit, and by falling down we show our servanthood and subjection. Then they add the psalms according to custom.

CHAPTER 14. THE 50TH PSALM

First they recite the 50th Psalm, as a psalm of confession and propitiation, as a petition for forgiveness of sins so that the Holy Spirit may not be taken away from us, but be renewed through humility and contrition of heart. We recite this psalm at the start of several services, since it speaks on the one hand of Adam and our whole race, and on the other hand of the Church gathered from the nations; the former was put to death because of lust and disobedience, the latter because at first she was unfaithful, committing adultery and spiritual murder like an apostate, but by God's mercy she was recalled and, receiving in abundance the Holy Spirit, was renewed.

CHAPTER 15. THE PSALMS OF THE 'BLAMELESS' [PS118]

After this they add the psalms of the 'Blameless' by verses, which bring to mind the kingdom of God, his judgments, statutes, testimonies, words and laws. These psalms are also recited at the commemoration of saints and for the faithful departed, since they refer to the memory of the saints and the path of the Savior. For he is the only one "blameless in the way," and by this means we his imitators propitiate God and are sanctified.

CHAPTER 16. WHY THE CREED IS RECITED MORNING AND EVENING

The Confession of Faith is said immediately after these psalms in accordance with patristic tradition, since the Fathers tells us: "Arise and praise God, then proclaim the faith." This most holy creed is the faith. Another of the venerable Fathers says that we should proclaim the faith morning and evening, so that if Death comes he will find us confessing. After the Confession of Faith we recite again the Trisagion and "Our Father," since we should praise the Holy Trinity always at every hour— at the beginning, in the middle and at the end— as the source of all things, and because everything is done through him and we are thereby perfected and purified.

Then "The Bridegroom Comes" indicates the aim of the Midnight Service of Praise. After this "Lord, have mercy" is recited forty times, this number signifying that we offer as a sacrifice to God a tithe of all the days and hours of our life. We do this at all the services, invoking the mercy of God before all things, for he alone can save us, since we have need of mercy. For we sin continually and cannot be saved by any other means than the mercy of God alone, not having anything in ourselves to propitiate him. We provoke him incessantly by our deeds, our words, our thoughts, so that we are not worthy even to thank him or praise him, nor to petition him for anything — but only to say "Lord, have mercy," hoping only in our merciful God.

After this, we invoke the Mother of God as "truly more honored than the Seraphim," for she is a powerful intercessor above all others. Then immediately the priest's prayer: "God have mercy upon us . . ." as the seal and completion, this prayer having been said by Moses to Aaron by divine command. The divine ancestor David also wrote it more clearly in Psalm 66.

After this, as confession to the Holy Trinity, we add another prayer which we say three times a day — at the Midnight Office, at the Third Hour, and at Compline. We find that this was sung by the ancients also, as in the passion of the Great Martyr Eustratios, i.e.: "O Lord God, Father Almighty; O Lord the only-begotten Son Jesus Christ, and Holy Spirit, etc."

Then we say a Mesorion [Intermediate Hour] to the Midnight Office, as some are accustomed to do with the services of the Hours. Let him recite other services also according to their wish and desire, as long as they are with the approval and judgment of the Fathers. My opinion is as follows:

I think that it was compiled as a prayer for the departed in Christ. Therefore, we say again "Come, let us fall down . . ." together with the prayer, two psalms, the prayer of the Trisagion, and then the Troparia for the Departed, "Lord, have mercy" twelve times, and the prayer for them: "Remember, O Lord . . ." Then the Dismissal takes place. It is necessary for us to commemorate the dead, since we also will die, and to commemorate them especially at the Midnight Office, for at this hour the resurrection of the dead is expected. We ought also to pray for our departed relatives and members of our household, and in general for all, as a work of charity. Then the common petition for all and the prayer, the priest beginning and the others continuing: "For faithful rulers, for Orthodox bishops, for the father abbot, for the brotherhood in Christ, and all other Christians . . ." Then again for our fathers and brothers who have died in the Orthodox faith.

It is most necessary that we commemorate all at the end of the prayers, since in this way we all pray for each other everywhere, and so it happens that we are healed and saved willy-nilly. The leader sets the seal on the common prayer, calling on Christ our God for mercy with "Through the prayers of our Holy Fathers. . ."

CHAPTER 17. THE SERVICE OF MATINS: FIRSTLY, THE SIGNIFICANCE OF THE OPENING OF THE SANCTUARY DOORS AND THE ENTRANCE AND CENSING

Thus, when the Midnight office is ended, the doors of the nave open like the heavens and we enter as from the earth, just as Christ's chosen will be taken up in clouds and be forever with the Lord. Like a cloud also the incense is offered, symbolizing the Holy Spirit and the transmission of his divine grace and fragrance. Then, when we have all entered — the leader through the Royal Door, which is closed to us, symbolizing the Theotokos, and which he opens to us like the gates of heaven, since he typifies Christ; the others from the sides, as his servants and under his wing— the priest as the minister of Christ gives the blessing from the sanctuary, blessing him with the Father and the Holy Spirit before his throne and his saints.

Then all sing the Trisagion and the God-given prayer, hymning the Holy Trinity with the angels. Regarding the prayer of the Trisagion, we should remind you in brief that this is an ancient prayer compiled by the early Fathers. For this reason the Church sings the Trisagion continually, both in the Holy Liturgy and at the end of the services, anathematizing certain heretics who made an addition to this hymn, while the Church — as from heaven through the boy taken up there — continually sings this heavenly and sweet melody.

The Trisagion and the whole prayer with it refers to the Holy Trinity, our only God, and derives both from the angelic hymn and from David: — from the angels because they sing holy, holy, holy; from David: "My soul thirsted for the Lord, the strong and living one" [Ps 41.3] — who also cries "have mercy upon me" in the 50th Psalm. This hymn proclaims continually the trinity of persons and the unity of the nature. Similarly also, "Most-holy Trinity, have mercy upon us" teaches the simultaneous trinity and unity: — "Lord be merciful . . ." refers to the Father; "Master, forgive . . ." to the Son; "Holy One, visit . . ." to the Holy Spirit. The indivisibility is expressed in saying "for thy name's sake." We rightly say to the Father "Be merciful," inasmuch as we have been reconciled to him through the Son; we rightly say to the Son "forgive," since he became human like us, suffered for us and all mankind, although provoked and grieved by us, the very people who have put him on in baptism and myron and have been united with him in Communion and the other sacraments. Again, we rightly say to him "forgive," for he himself granted the power to loose and to bind, and established forgiveness. We rightly say "visit" to the Holy Spirit, for he gives us life and strengthens us, and without his power and gift there would be no good in us.

"Lord, have mercy" also proclaims the Holy Trinity, for the Holy Trinity is One Lord, and in repeating it thrice we testify and request mercy. Similarly also, "Glory to the Father and to the Son and to the Holy Spirit" is a clear confession and doxology of the same Holy Trinity, sung perpetually to God. For this reason we sing it continually, at the start and the finish of the hymns. Similarly also, "Our Father"— even though it is addressed to the Father and was given to us by the Son. Since, however, the Holy Trinity is indivisible and there is one name of the Father and of the Son and of the Holy Spirit, and one God — because the Father is the father of lights, of the Son and of the Holy Spirit, and is in the Son and the Holy Spirit, and the Son and Holy Spirit in the Father — therefore this prayer is addressed to God, and in saying "Father" it calls to mind the Son and the Holy Spirit also. The Church also witnesses to this in saying: "For yours is the kingdom, of the Father and of the Son and of the Holy Spirit."

Let us return now to our subject. When, as we said, the priest has given the blessing, he censes the sanctuary, the nave and all present, since all things are sanctified — the things he censes, as being holy; the people present, to sanctify them. Thus, beginning at the Holy of Holies, the sanctuary, he censes everything in order. However, he does not cense them simply as by chance, but he seals and sanctifies and offers the sanctification to Christ, so that it may become acceptable in heaven, and that the grace of the all-holy Spirit may be sent upon us. For this reason let nobdy neglect the censing, since through it he receives the grace of the Holy Spirit.

Having passed fairly quickly through the whole nave and what is beyond it by the end of the Lord's prayer, he enters the gates and making the sign of the cross with the censer says: "For yours is the kingdom . . . ," sealing the prayer as Christ said, and praising the Holy Trinity. Then he censes the presiding cleric a second time, giving him honor as to Christ, whom he typifies. He also censes the holy icons in the center, and entering the sanctuary stands before the Holy Table as before the divine throne and holy tomb of Christ. When the people outside have said "Bless, Father," he sings aloud with devotion and fervor "Glory to the holy and consubstantial and life-giving and indivisible and almighty Trinity always . . . ," theologizing thus on the cause and master of all, the only God in Trinity, and praising him before every Canticle and at the end of all the hymns as the origin and end of all. Then, when "amen" has been said, an affirming particle equivalent to "yes," and all are silent in imitation of the piety and silence of the angels at the fearful mysteries of God, one of those present appointed for this and typifying the angel sent from God introduces the song of the angels which lauded the birth of Christ, which one angel appearing to the shepherd originally sang, and immediately a multitude of the heavenly host appeared singing: "Glory to God on high" [Lk 2.13-14] — which is the first fruits of praise to the angels for our salvation.

Therefore, here also in imitation of that, one of us introduces this by saying thrice to the glory of the all-praised Trinity, "Glory to God on high," then twice "Lord, you will open my lips . . ." [Ps 50.17]. He says this thrice again in honor of the Holy Trinity. Then "Lord, how are they multiplied that oppress me" [Ps 3] and the other five psalms of the Hexapsalmos, praising the remembrance of the Holy Trinity after each three psalms, while the priest offers to God the Matins Prayers, as a mediator with God through what is said, completing what is sung, for everything is completed by the priesthood. For this reason it is always the priest who begins and ends.

Then, as soon as the priest has offered the Matins Prayers to God, he recites the Litany of Peace (after the end of the Hexapsalmos) and prays for everyone; and then all the lights are lit, signifying that the glory of the Lord shone about them. "God the Lord . . ." is sung aloud melodically in imitation of the glorifying angels. Most proper and appropriate is "God the Lord has appeared also to us, " i.e., the Word of God became incarnate; "Blessed is he that comes" — God himself as through the flesh; "in the name of the Lord"—of the Father and of himself, that is.

Then, if it is a feast day, the hymns of the feast are sung, or if a commemoration of some saint, those of the saint, for through the Incarnate One human nature has also been sanctified.

Fittingly the Nativity and Epiphany in the flesh of the Savior are typified at night, for they took place by night, and "on us sitting in darkness and the shadow of ignorance the great light has shone" [Is 9.2]. For this reason we also who

behave in this life as though we were in the night waiting for
the beloved and desired bridegroom of our souls to come to us.

Then the reading from the Psalter takes place, with a
Doxology and Alleluia after each three psalms. The Holy
Trinity is glorified by the "Glory be to the Father . . ." and
the incarnation of the Word by the Alleluia, which means
"God comes," signifying by this his presence on earth, which
first took place in the flesh and in poverty, but later will be
awaited from heaven in glory.

Readings from holy discourses are also added for the
teaching of the mystery and praise of the saints commemorated. For even in that bright festival of the coming age, the
mysteries of God will be glorified, and especially that of his
becoming man, whether glorified alone or together with the
heroic deeds of those who fought the good fight for him— as
happens also at the victory celebrations of kings, where we
see proclaimed and crowned with wreaths those who fought
victoriously for them, as Chrysostom mentions in several
passages.

After the reading is sung the hymn of the Polyeleos
[Ps 134.5] , a triumphal song recounting the wonderful deeds
of God, especially the passing over from Egypt (i.e., from the
sin and error of our souls to the faith of Christ); and our being
freed from Pharaoh and the Egyptians (i.e., from the Devil
and the demons); and the orderly march from the sea of life's
temptations over dry land (i.e., the strong and calm life in the
power of God and patience in afflictions) as strengthened by
the staff (i.e., with the power of the Cross and baptism). Or
again, our being freed from a life of tribulation as in the
desert through our sloth and negligence in fulfilling the divine
commands and through our complaining to God because of
our afflictions, even though we are nourished with the bread
of life incomparably greater than manna, and watered with
the spring of blood from Christ's side. Or similarly, the
saving of the Church from the persecution of Diocletian,
Maximin, the Apostate, and other most impious tyrants—
(like that of the Israelites from Amalek, Sion, and Og)—since
the rule of those infidels coincided with the tyranny of the
demons, through whom afflictions were visited on the world,

and the various temptations of the saints, in short from temptations and griefs — the occupation and inheriting of the promised land, which is heaven, through Jesus the Son of the living God, who also will make us heir and inheritors, and transport us into the heavenly Jerusalem. As Great High priest he grants us the priesthood and the living sacrifice, and as sole king he will put in order the coming kingdom which will have no end.

After the chants, other selections from the psalms are sung appropriate for the feasts of the saints, which are also proclamations of the miracles of God, and the priest then proclaims the Gospel which seals and presents all the mysteries. Through this mystery which was manifested, the section is completed and triumphal hymns are sung to the Kanons.

CHAPTER 18. THE NINE CANTICLES (ODES) WHICH ARE SUNG TO THE KANONS

Then are sung the Canticles which were chanted by the holy prophets.

The first Canticle is that of Miriam the sister, of Moses, for the passing over of Israel.

The second is of Moses, after the crossing of the desert.

The third is a thanksgiving prayer of Hannah after the removal of her sterility and bearing the holy fruit of Samuel — as a prototype of the Church, which was first barren but later cultivated and by command bore priests like Samuel, kings appointed by priests like David, and their descendants the apostles, the hierarchs, and the kings of Christendom appointed through them.

The fourth is that of Habbakuk, who saw God coming from Thaiman, from the mountain of shadow, i.e., from the east — the unsetting sun of righteousness, Christ, coming from the Virgin.

The fifth is of Isaiah, who prophesied the wonder: "Behold the virgin will conceive and bear a son, and you will call his name Emmanuel" [Is 7.14], and also prophesied the other things concerning the Beloved One and the resurrection of the dead.

The sixth is the Canticle of Jonah, a prototype of him who was buried and rose on the third day, through the sea-monster.

The seventh is a song of the Three Youths to God, who as a type of the divine incarnation, were not consumed in the furnace.

The eighth is a doxology of those Youths to God, whom they glorify with the whole of creation, clearly manifesting that all the world recognizes and believes in God, who condescended to us and bedewed them in the furnace as a type of the most-holy baptism.

The ninth is a prophecy of Zachariah concerning his son at his birth, who was named and served as the prelude and forerunner of grace. With this is also the most excellent of all, the most prophetic, theological, sacred and blessed Canticle of the outstandingly pure and holy Theotokos, most glorious Mary, recited regarding her immaculate birth-giving, by which He who was incarnate of her adopted us as the New Israel, as he had promised to Abraham.

These nine Canticles, then, the Church sings daily as a triple type of the most divine Trinity, as triumphal and thanksgiving hymns to the Kanons, in these three sections honoring the Holy Trinity also, whom the priest praises as one after the completion of the third Canticle.

CHAPTER 19. THE KATHISMATA [SESSION-HYMNS]

Then when the discourses of the saints regarding the feast are read as common teaching, they sit down and sing sitting — on the one hand for a little bodily rest, on the other hand because we should praise God whether sitting or standing.

CHAPTER 20. THE KONTAKION AND IKOS

Similarly, after the sixth Canticle, when the priest has sung his doxology, the Kontakion is recited as a concise extolling of the feast in one troparion; and what is called the Ikos is also recited, since it contains all the details of the feast or the life of the saint, and is chanted at the end of the Kontakion with a slight melody. Then what is called the Synaxarion is read, since it contains in brief the details of the feast or of the saints commemorated on that day, covering in short form both the feast celebrated and the heroic deeds of the others, praising each of them in iambic verses.

After the eighth Canticle, at the start of the ninth, we magnify her who was indeed above all the saints, the Theotokos in whom God truly did great miracles, becoming incarnate of her and showing her to whom the holy ode refers to be higher than the Seraphim and Cherubim. At the end of the ninth Canticle the priest praises the Holy Trinity as the angels do.

CHAPTER 21. THE EXAPOSTEILARION, THE LAUDS PSALMS (AINOI) AND THE GREAT DOXOLOGY

It is called Exaposteilarion because of "Send forth your light" and is recited as a light-bringer before the Lauds Psalms.

Then the Lauds Psalms [Ps 148-150] are added, calling all creation, the angels and all creatures to the praise of the Creator, and witnessing that all creatures are the works of God, created in word and spirit. "For he spoke and they were created," it is written, "He commanded and they were made" [Ps 148.5]. "Spoke" here means through the word; "commanded" means through the operation of the Holy Spirit.

After the appropriate hymns to the Lauds Psalms and "Glory be to the Father . . ." and "Now and ever . . ." in honor of the Holy Trinity, the Great Doxology is performed. This is that "Glory to God on high" which we mentioned at the beginning. Here it is sung by all more fully and with melody, for the mystery was revealed to the whole world and not to the shepherds only, but to all the nations as well. Therefore we say: "We praise you, we bless you, we worship you, we glorify you, we thank you for your great glory," because heaven is full of his glory and so is earth. Whose glory?—that of God in Trinity. Thus the Church theologizes in crying: "O Lord, King, heavenly God, Father almighty; O Lord, only-begotten Son Jesus Christ, and Holy Spirit . . ." See that it has preached the three persons in one Divinity; in saying "we praise you" it manifests the unity of God who is on high, while by the number it proclaims the persons. Then we solemnly praise the incarnation of God, chanting: "O Lord God, Lamb of God," taking this from Isaiah and the Forerunner because of his passion and sacrifice; "Son of the Father" —from the Gospel; "who takes away the sin of the world, have mercy upon us, you who take away the sin of the world, and receive our prayer"—this also from Isaiah; "You who sit at the right of the Father, and have mercy upon us"—this gleaned from the Gospel; "receive" and "have mercy" from David; "For you alone are holy, you alone are Lord, Jesus Christ, in the glory of God the Father, Amen." — from Paul; "Every day I will praise you and extol your name forever and ever" — from the divine David. The remainder is made up of petitions and prophetic verses.

CHAPTER 22. THE TRISAGION HYMN

Finally, the Trisagion Hymn is said, being the seal and completion of every hymn, since it refers to the one God, to the Holy Trinity: "Holy God, holy and mighty, holy and immortal, have mercy upon us." As we said above, this hymn was originally composed by the holy Fathers and is called Great Doxology. Each of the faithful should study and learn and recite it every morning and evening to God, since it is both a confession and doxology of the Holy Trinity, the one God, and a commemoration of the incarnation and dispensation, crucifixion and resurrection of one person of the Holy Trinity, of the Word of God; an acceptable prayer that we may be preserved sinless all day and night; that we may be made worthy of the divine mercy, as we hope; that he may have pity on us; therefore we cry with David: "Have mercy and heal my soul, for I have sinned against you" [Ps 40.5] — behold the confession; and "for I took refuge with you" (the refuge of all) and "teach me to do your will, for you are my God" [Ps 142.9-10], the Father together with the Son and the Holy Spirit. For this reason is added "with you is the spring of life" (the Holy Spirit), "in your light" (i.e., in your Spirit) "we

shall see light" (that is, the Son), "Extend your mercy to
those who know you" [Ps 13.11] — you, the true God and
Father with the Word and your Holy Spirit through the incarnation of your Son. The Trisagion Hymn is added.

CHAPTER 23. THE MEANING OF THE ANGELIC HYMN: HOLY, HOLY, HOLY, ETC.

The Trisagion Hymn is sung by the angels, as we have learnt
from Isaiah, in the following way: "Holy, Holy, Holy, Lord
of Sabaoth: heaven and earth are full of your glory" [Is.6] .
As we have learnt from Athanasios the Great and the other
Fathers, the meaning is this: the Father is holy, the Son is
holy, the Holy Spirit is holy — behold the three persons; "Lord
of Sabaoth" — behold the unity of the Godhead, the unique-
ness of the nature and the oneness of the glory. "Holy" is said
three times because of the three persons, "Lord once because
of the one Divinity, and "heaven and earth are full of your
glory" because of the knowledge of the Holy Trinity, the
thrice-holy God. This knowledge was granted by divine dispensation, through the angels and apostles of Christ; and
heaven and earth became full of this dispensation. The hymn
states "full of your glory" in the singular, for there is one
glory of the Holy Trinity, one power, one will, one movement
and operation, and one God alone in Trinity.

CHAPTER 24. THE EXPLANATION OF THE TRISAGION: HOLY GOD, HOLY AND MIGHTY, HOLY AND IMMORTAL HAVE MERCY ON US

Therefore, the Fathers orginally received from the angels
the "Holy, Holy, Holy," and from David the remainder, where
he glorifies God in Trinity saying: "My soul thirsted for
God, the mighty One, the living One" [Ps 41.3] , and rightly
and most appropriately composed the Trisagion Hymn. As
a mark of petition they added — again from David — the "have
mercy upon us." So they say "Holy God . . . — the "holy" from
the angels, the "God" from David; "Holy (and) Mighty" — similarly the "holy" is angelic, the "mighty" Davidic; "Holy

(and) Immortal" —"holy " from the angels, while they took the "immortal" from David instead of "living"; the "have mercy upon us" similarly from David, for he also spoke in the Holy Spirit, as the Savior witnesses: "David said in the Spirit" [Mt 22.43]. Consequently, they applied the "God" to the Father, since he is the spring and root of the divinity and source of the Son and the Holy Spirit; the "mighty" was applied to the Son as arm and power of the Father personified — "For Christ is the power of God and the wisdom of God," says Paul [1 Cor 1.24] ; the "immortal" was applied to the Holy Spirit, since life belongs to the Holy Spirit" — "The Spirit is the life-giver," it is said; and since God is mighty and living, both his power is mighty and his life immortal.

CHAPTER 25. AGAINST PETER THE FULLER

A great and foolish attack has been made by the heretics through a certain person of ill-fame, Peter the Fuller, who wished to add to this hymn to the Holy Trinity, who is incapable of suffering: "who was crucified for us." Such an addition was extremely blasphemous, since the Holy Trinity is incapable of suffering, infinite and incorporeal. Only one person of the Trinity, God the Word, suffered — not in his divinity, but in the flesh, since the divinity remained incapable of suffering and uncrucified; just as when iron is beaten and suffers while incandescent, the fire does not suffer with it, nor is it changed, but it illumines and fires the iron, as Saint Basil says. However, this heresy—after lighting fiery temptations for the Church for a long time—was quenched again by the power of God through a miracle which took place in the Christ-loving city of Constantine during the reign of Theodosios the Younger. While the Church was holding a procession, a boy was caught up into midair and came down crying that the angels recite it "Holy God, Holy and Mighty, Holy and Immortal: have mercy upon us," and then died. You see therefore that the Church received this Trisagion Hymn not only from the prophets, but also from its children in the Holy Spirit. God the Trinity witnessed also that this hymn is sung ceaselessly by the angels to the same Trinity.

For this reason, having received it from God, who settled the upheaval on earth by the correct formulation of the hymn, the Church always sings it with the angels at all times of prayer, especially with divine melody as in the Great Doxology at the end of Matins and in the Holy Liturgy. The Great Doxology is, therefore, sung daily, on feasts, and commemorations of saints — according to the Typikon; on other days it is read penitentially by one person, with the prayer of the Trisagion afterwards—as we will discuss briefly to answer your question.

CHAPTER 26. THE TRISAGION AND A SECOND INTERPRETATION OF THE PRAYER "OUR FATHER"

This prayer is recited both at the start and in the middle of each service, and often at the end, since it refers entirely to our one God in Trinity, deriving its beginning from the angelic hymn and its end from the Lord's Prayer. You know the arrangement of the prayer, and it contains this significance: the Trisagion is said thrice as a triple remembrance of the Holy Trinity.

CHAPTER 27. THE "GLORY BE TO THE FATHER AND TO THE SON AND TO THE HOLY SPIRIT," AND BY WHOM IT WAS COMPOSED

Another hymn composed by the Fathers is sung to the glory of the Holy Trinity, as some say by Meletios and Flavianos the patriarchs of Antioch among the saints. "Glory be to the Father and to the Son and to the Holy Spirit, both now and forever and to the ages of ages, Amen." This was piously composed against Arios and Sabellios, the "Glory" being aimed against the Arians, since the glory of the Holy Trinity is one and the Trinity is consubstantial, while "to the Father and to the Son and to the Holy Spirit" was composed against Sabellios, who blasphemously claimed that there is one person in the Holy Trinity; and "both now and forever..."

because it is so and will be so forever.

Then "Most-holy Trinity, have mercy upon us," this prayer also composed by the Fathers. First it proclaims the three
persons together, since their divinity, power and essence are
one and the Holy Trinity is indivisible. Then it mentions the
number of the persons through the characteristics of the
Father: "O Lord, have mercy towards our sins"; of the Son:
"O Master, forgive our transgression"; of the most-holy
Spirit: "O Holy One, visit and heal our infirmities": then
again it manifests the unity of the three persons: "for your
name's sake." The Father is Lord because the Son is Lord
and the Spirit is Lord also, through consubstantiality; and
there is one lordship of the three, and the Holy Trinity is one
Lord only; the Son is Master because the Father rules all
together with the Holy Spirit; the Spirit is holy because the
Father and the Son are holy also. The "Lord, have mercy" is
gleaned from David; "be merciful towards our sins" is a
saying of the Publican, from the Gospel; "forgive our transgressions" is also from the Gospel, from "forgive us (our
trespasses)," and from the Prophets and the Fathers; "visit
and heal our infirmities, is again from the Gospel and the
Psalms; similarly, "for your name's sake" is from the Psalms.
Then "Lord, have mercy" three times, in honor of the Holy
Trinity. For the Holy Trinity is one Lord, so that we say
"Holy, Holy, Holy, Lord . . . ," and say it thrice because of
the Holy Trinity. Then again, "Glory be to the Father . . . ,"
etc. for the Holy Trinity is of one glory. Finally, the Lord's
Prayer, the meaning of which we will interpret briefly to the
best of our ability.

CHAPTER 28. A BRIEF EXPOSITION OF THE MOST HOLY PRAYER "OUR FATHER"

"Our Father": We call the God of heaven "Father" as
maker and creator, since he formed us from nothing; and he
is our Father, indeed, by grace, since his Son — only-begotten
by nature — became man for our salvation.

"Who are in heaven": Being holy, as he is called in the sacred Scriptures, God is pleased and rests in his saints. The angels in heaven are holier than we humans, and heaven is purer than earth; therefore, God is mentioned in heaven rather than on earth.

"May your name be hallowed": Since you are holy, O God, sanctify your revered name among us also, and sanctify and cleanse us from every stain, so that we may be sanctified and become your own through our purity; and preach your holy name, so that it may be glorified always through us and not be cursed by us humans.

"May your kingdom come": May you be king over us because of our good and virtuous works, and not your enemy the Devil because of our evil and lawless works. And may your heavenly kingdom come, i.e., the last day of the world, since you will then reign over all—even over your enemies. And may your kingdom be eternal, as it is now. May it be a spring of grace for those who are worthy, virtuous and prepared for the time of your kingdom with their good works, but also punitive towards your foes.

"May your will be done, on earth as it is in heaven": Like the angels, make us perform it among us as your will is among them. Let not our will be done, since we are passionate and human, but your own dispassionate will, just and holy. Since by the incarnation of your only-begotten Son you united the heavenly and earthly spheres, may your heavenly wishes be executed in us also who are on earth.

"Give us today our daily bread": Even though we have sought the heavenly work, since the whole hope of us Christians is towards the heavenly life, yet being mortal and human we also seek the sustaining bread to support our life, while knowing well that it can only be given by your hand; you alone are self-sufficient, whereas we are subject to needs and necessity. Since we have confidence and hope in you alone, we do not seek something superfluous in seeking that bread, but only what satisfies our current needs and necessity; for we have been taught in the Gospels not to take thought for the morrow, since you who are provident for us today will also be so tomorrow and forever. "Give us today our essential bread" signifies also the living, heavenly bread, the most holy body of the living Word, our Savior Christ. It is called essential because it strengthens both our souls and bodies. Whoever does not eat this has no life in Christ, but whoever eats of it will live the heavenly and unaging life forever.

"And forgive us our debts, as we forgive our debtors": In this is contained all the wisdom and power of the sacred gospel, for it was primarily to forgive our sins and trespasses that the Word of God, our loving Savior, came into the world and became incarnate, sharing all the things of mankind except sin, and finally shed his pure blood. For this reason he gave us the sacrament of Holy Communion for forgiveness of sins, teaching us and legislating clearly, "If you forgive, you will be forgiven" [Mt 6.I4]. For this reason also he said to Peter when he asked him: "How many times a day should I forgive my brother?" [Mt 18.21]. He replied up to seventy times i.e., unceasingly. In this sacred prayer God appoints the person praying to be his own judge. If we make peace with whoever has grieved us, God also will make peace with us: ". . . he forgave and it will be forgiven him" [Lk 17.3]. We must not bear grudges or want revenge at all costs against our brothers who have offended us, for this is the will of our Lord and Savior; we being all similar as humans, subject to error and granting little forgiveness to sinners because of our self-love, although we receive much from God and are forgiven often. If we forgive other humans, we also are forgiven by God.

"And lead us not into temptation": This is said because there are many who tempt us, full of envy and emnity, and many are the temptations that come—from the demons, from mankind, from the body, from negligence, in short from spiritual sloth. These temptations afflict both the careful and the careless, the virtuous and the wicked. The only difference is that the temptations of the righteous have more reward from God, because they occur to test and exalt us, as with Job, and also because these righteous persons have greater need of patience, since they are afflicted more by being envied and hated in the world: Their "spirit is willing, but the flesh is weak" [Mt 26.41]. There are also other temptations, such as rejecting and neglecting your brother in tribulations, persecuting him, oppressing him, and neglecting or despising the divine things. So, whatever sins and faults we may have committed against God and our brother, we need only beg mercy from God, have mercy and forgive others, driving temptations and evil away from us—immediately we enjoy forgiveness and mercy. However, if somebody is righteous, he should, nonetheless, not have confidence in himself, because being righteous consists primarily in humbling oneself and in being merciful and forgiving to others.

"But deliver us from evil": Save us from evil, from the Devil who is our mortal and untiring enemy, possessed by a mania, for without God's grace we are powerless against him, since he is a spirit of subtle nature and cunning, inventing and devising a myriad of evils against us daily. If you, the Creator and Master of All — of the wicked Devil and other evil powers also, as you are of the angels and us humans — if you did not snatch us away from the temptations of the Devil, who else could save us? Since we have no power to resist an incorporeal enemy who is alway so envious, crafty and scheming, you alone save us from him!

"For yours is the kingdom and the power and the glory forever, Amen": Who could hurt us and afflict us, when we are ruled by you, the God and king and lord of all, the commander of the angels themselves? Or who could oppose your power? Nobody since, you created us and protect us all. Or who could contradict or dare to do anything against your glory, when this glory commands the furthermost limits, and heaven and earth are filled by it, being more ancient than the heavens and the angels, for you alone existed always and are eternal. May your glory—of the Father and of the Son and of the Holy Spirit—and your kingdom and power be eternal, amen. For you are truly and confessedly the king, the mighty and glorified One forever.

This is, in brief, the power of the Trisagion and the sacred prayer "Our Father." Every Orthodox Christian should know this prayer—no excuses!—and offer it to God, both when he leaves his house and when he enters the holy temple of God, before and after meals, and in the evening when going to sleep, because this prayer of Trisagion and "Our Father" contains confession and glorification of God, humbling of the person praying, revelation of his sins, requesting of forgiveness, hope in heavenly benefits to come, requesting of necessary things and renunciation of unnecessary ones, hope in God and the wish that temptation may be driven from us, that we may be saved from evil and execute God's holy will, and be his children — as we are by grace — and may finally be made worthy of his kingdom. This is why the Church offers this prayer to God many times each day. You see that we have discussed this in detail as best we could—now we must add the conclusion of Matins, in Christ.

CHAPTER 29. WHY WE REQUEST MERCY IN THE PRAYERS, AND BEFORE EACH SERVICE

On feasts after the Great Doxology, or on ordinary days after the prayer of the Trisagion and the Lord's Prayer, the priest performs the intercession, in which firstly and principally we request God's mercy and divine pity from our merciful God, saying: "Have mercy upon us, O God, according to your great mercy, we beseech you," etc. This intercession is appropriate, since we should not ask for anything except for mercy, as we have neither boldness nor access to offer anything as our own, nor to request anything as such, since everything is from God and of God, nor can we think that we have not sinned.

So, as sinners and condemned through sin we cannot, nor dare not, say anything to our loving Master except "have mercy." For we have grieved him and grieve him every day, so much that we cannot cry anything except "have mercy," both priest and people together, while the priest says: "Have mercy upon us, O God, according to your great mercy: we beseech you, hear and have mercy." What does this mean, "we beseech you, hear and have mercy?" We cry that we are not worthy to be heard and pitied, because of the multitude of our faults, so we beseech you, i.e., we ask you to hear our prayers and have mercy upon us. As mediator, the priest stands before God and says "we beseech you" and "hear us," while the people add the petition "Lord, have mercy." For it is your great love for mankind, O God, that you have mercy, and the fitting petition and request of us sinners is the "Lord, have mercy." For this reason before every other prayer the priest says: "Let us beseech the Lord," i.e., let us beg of the Lord. Those present show that this is a petition for the divine mercy by crying: "Lord, have mercy," at the same time assisting the priests, for the petition of the righteous has great power with God.

You see then the humble wisdom and order of our Church? You see how it sets in order and offers its children to God through penitence and humility? We do not perceive this, brethren, nor do we understand these lofty meanings, but only speak with our lips by habit, and are in a hurry to shake off prayer as a burden. Others out of indolence do not say the "have mercy," nor do we attend with our mind when it is recited, and therefore do not receive God's mercy. Ponder and reflect on the aim of the Church, however, and attend to this aim— both you and other pious persons so that you may receive mercy from God.

Cleric: I understand, holy master, and surprised at your words I shrink, because although we have been made worthy of such gifts beyond our merits we do not appreciate them at all.

Archbishop: May God, who adorned mankind with wisdom, grant us understanding, strengthen us and have mercy upon us. Know that in the evening services and in the Holy Liturgy the Church does not refrain from teaching and inciting us to understand, which is why it adds: "Let us all say . . . with all our mind let us say . . . ," etc.

CHAPTER 30. THE SIGNIFICANCE OF "WISDOM," AND LET US ATTEND," AND "WISDOM, BE UPSTANDING."

"Let us all say . . ." and what follows is an incitement and teaching, as is "Wisdom," "Let us attend" and "Wisdom, be upstanding," i.e., all be upstanding in wisdom, for what is said and done is the wisdom of God, and belongs to God's living wisdom. Since "The fear of the Lord is the beginning of wisdom" [Prov 1.7] let us be with wisdom and piety when we see and hear the divine things; let us attend to them with the fear of God; let us stand upright in wisdom, both in body and soul, upright in faith and thoughts. Do you understand how much wisdom the details of the Church contain, which seem trifling to us?

Cleric: I understand and am amazed, master.

Archbishop: Do not be amazed, brother, because the Church is the dwelling of the living wisdom of God personified, which is why "Wisdom has built herself a house" [Pr 9-4] — the sacred body of the Church. This is why those details of this Church which seem trifling are full of wisdom; and the smaller some people think them, the greater the knowledge and understanding required. For the things of God which seem foolish to mankind are very wise, and those which seem weak are very strong, and the living wisdom of God is one and simple. In it are to be found all the treasures of wisdom and knowledge.

After the intercessions come the petitions and bowing of the head, when all bow their heads and stand in silence, signifying the enormous reverence due to God from us, and manifestation of our servanthood and subjection. When the priest has besought God, the only holy Lord dwelling in the heights of his glory and surveying all, of whom we have subjected both our bodies and souls — when he has besought divine blessing, forgiveness of our voluntary and involuntary sins, worldly and other-worldly benefits, he raises his head as strengthened by God. The priest, rising with the people, thanks God and chants: "For it is yours to have mercy and save . . . ," and performs the Dismissal. Again he says "Wisdom," to arouse us to hear the following prayer.

What is this prayer, "Blessed be our God, the Existent, always?" This is from the book of Moses and signifies that God exists eternal and unchanged, and is the saying of God Himself: "I AM that I AM, and I AM has sent me" [Ex 3.14]. Then we invoke her who is more honored than the angels, the Theotokos, since she is a more powerful intercessor for us with God, and the priest says: "Most holy Theotokos, help us." Finally, when all have chanted as a final doxology to the Holy Trinity: "Glory be to the Father and to the Son and to the Holy Spirit," the priest adds the conclusion of Matins with a prayer called Dismissal. This is a permission, since nobody is allowed to leave the divine services without the permission of the priest. Thus as the priest began the service, so he also gives the conclusion and places the seal on the prayers.

CHAPTER 31. THE PRAYER OF THE DISMISSAL

The seal, i.e., the dismissal, is none other than he who became incarnate for us, Christ the true God; as his beloved disciple John says: "He is the true God and life eternal" [Jn 14.6]. When the priest has invoked the intercessions of his holy Mother and all the saints—since this is a sign of His extreme goodness, that he became man with a mother and a choir of saints, i.e., those who have pleased him — he says: "Have mercy upon us and save us."

This, indeed, said appropriately, since God became man for our sake and took his mother and all the saints from our human race. Then we perform the prayers for our deceased founders and fathers, to whom we owe something. It is essential to remember them, since we are descended from them and will be set with them, and our Savior did not suffer and die on the Cross for the living only but also for the departed. Great benefit is derived from these commemorations, both for those commemorated and for us who commemorate them. This commemoration takes place after the service of the First Hour.

CHAPTER 32. THE FIRST HOUR

The service of praise for the First Hour is performed immediately after the Dismissal of Matins if it is a festival, or joined to Matins with the Dismissal later, since it is one service of praise with Matins, as we said above. We say: "Come, let us worship our king, Christ our God" three times, for he is our only and eternal king, by nature Lord alone with the Father and the Spirit, and has destroyed the power and tyranny of the Devil and freed us from darkness and death. Then we say three psalms in honor of the Trinity—those said by David in the morning as thanks to God—that the divine radiance may come upon us, that our works may be guided, and that we may be preserved from all evil and filled with all goodness.

After the psalms, troparia with the same import, and another one to the Mother of God, with the angel proclaiming her most blessed; heaven, because she brought forth the Sun of righteousness; paradise, because she gave birth to Christ, the tree of life; virgin, because she remains ever-virgin. It is fittingly recited at this time, because of the perceptible rising of the sun, and because paradise is in the east. Then the praise of the Trisagion and "Our Father," since it is impossible not to remember this at every hour.

CHAPTER 33. WHY AT EACH HOUR AND OTHER SERVICES THERE IS A FORTY-FOLD "LORD, HAVE MERCY"

"Lord, have mercy " is said forty times as a sanctification of each season of our lives. Because forty days is one-tenth of the 365 days, or as some say, because the Great Fast lasts forty days: at every service we say "Lord, have mercy" forty times to wipe out our indescribable sins at every hour. For this reason we always recite the most necessary prayer, i.e., "You who at every season and hour" after "Lord, have mercy." By this we seek from God sanctification of our souls, bodies, thoughts, concerns and deeds, and beseech Him that we may be delivered from all temptation, and that guarded by the holy angels we may come to the knowledge and understanding of the glory of God, i.e., to the enjoyment in operation of the unapproachable radiance and grace of God, who is blessed to all ages. Then we praise the Theotokos as more honored than the Seraphim, and the priest recites the prayer given to Aaron for the people and recorded by David, i.e., "God have mercy upon us" [Ps 66.2]. Then immediately the prayer pertaining to the first hour, "Christ, the true light," is recited and the dismissal is added by the priest.

CHAPTER 34. THE OTHER HOURS—THIRD, SIXTH AND NINTH— WITH THE FIRST HOUR

The Third and Sixth Hours are sung similarly to the First, with various psalms and troparia as customary, except that the Trisagion is said before the Third after the priest gives the blessing, plus "Lord, have mercy" twelve times. The Trisagion is said also at the Ninth Hour, Compline, and Matins, since it refers primarily to the Holy Trinity, as does the Lord's Prayer. The twelve-fold "Lord, have mercy" is said because there are twelve hours of the day and of the night, for our sanctification and purification from whatever faults we may have committed, whether in word or deed, during those Hours — just as we say "Lord, have mercy" forty times at each Hour for the reasons stated above.

CHAPTER 35. THE PSALMS OF THE THIRD, SIXTH, AND NINTH HOURS

At each Hour, i.e., at the First, Third, Sixth, and Ninth, we say "Come, let us worship" three times in honor of the Holy Trinity and as an expression of the mystery of that hour. As the First Hour contains the psalms referring to the morning and the divine brightness from the rekindling of the sunrise, so those of the Third refer to the guile of the Jews and their hostility to Christ. The last one, called the 50th, refers to the indwelling of the Holy Spirit. Those of the Sixth Hour show the revolt of the Jews and their seeking the soul of the Lord and his death, since at this sixth hour they crucified him. They describe also how they grieved the Lord with their blows, their insults, their manic anger and hostility, and how the earth shook and darkness covered it, etc. The last psalm of the Sixth Hour reveals the assistance of the Father in distress, since it reads "He who dwells in the assistance of the Highest," and his victory over Hades — "He will tread upon the asp and the basilisk" [Ps 90].

The psalms of the Ninth Hour show the salvation of the human race which took place through the death of Christ and the slaying of His holy body; and that God is alive, even though he died in the flesh for our sake and became a sacrifice for us, to assist not only the living but also the dead in Hades, in the place of lamentation; and that favor came to the earth, the independent will of God, freeing our souls from the captivity of the Devil and forgiving our faults. With this release from captivity he brought us to life, who were dead by sin, and heartened his people through his resurrection, and preached peace and mercy. Truth recovered, and justice came forth from heaven, for by his death Jesus Christ abolished death. The final psalm, "Incline Lord," [Ps 85], signifies all this, i.e., he is holy and sinless who was crucified, died and rose for us; merciful, forgiving and faithful; and he has given power to us and to himself. To himself, in that he became the son of his handmaiden, i.e., the Mother of God; to us, in that he granted us a sign of goodness, his honored cross and resurrection. Through this sign also his enemies have been vanquished. Then we recite troparia and so forth, and finally — as we said above — the priest adds prayers appropriate to the hour.

Vespers is performed with all these things in this way. However, before these Hours the Third-Sixth Hour (*Trithekte*) and the so-called Typika are sung. Consider, brother, the harmony, the great and pious wisdom of the holy Church.

Since reciting the praise of the Hours continually at intervals and with interruptions causes some lukewarmness and carelessness, especially to the souls of the less perfect, our holy fathers—enlightened by the divine Spirit—devised the following arrangement, so that all the Hours are completed at three times. For with this arrangement they are concerned that all the doxologies are performed in succession and not in confusion, and at the same time to correct the lukewarmness, i.e., the lack of care and consideration among those present.

CHAPTER 36. WE ARE WELL-ADVISED TO COMPLETE ALL THE SERVICES AT THREE TIMES IN HONOR OF THE HOLY TRINITY AND TO AVOID CARELESSNESS

The holy Fathers ordered all the services at three indispensable and necessary times to the glory and honor of our God, the supersubstantial Holy Trinity.

The first time of services was set between midnight and dawn, with three services to be recited in this period. This was ordered for the manifestation and glory of the Holy Trinity. These three services are: the Midnight Office, Matins and Prime (although the latter is essentially only one joined with Matins, and not counted with the seven services of praise).

After the third hour of the day, three services are again performed for the glorification of the most holy and supersubstantial Trinity. After the third hour of the day the service for this hour and that for the sixth are sung together with that of the Typika—although the order of the Typika is not part of the seven praises, but always sung with the Sixth or Ninth Hour, and is a special and separate service, which we will shortly discuss in brief.

The service of the Ninth, plus Vespers and Compline, is performed towards the end of the day, and is similarly divided into three, manifesting the Holy Trinity, although sung united and consecutively at one time.

Thus three times were appointed in each twenty-four-hour period, with three services of praise at each time. In these three times the Church imitates the good Daniel who prayed to God three times every day, as is written in the Visions [Dan 6.5]. With the three services at each of the three times during the twenty-four-hour period, the Church aims at glorifying the Holy Trinity in imitation of the nine orders of angels, who in their number — three triads — praise God fervently and unceasingly.

CHAPTER 37. THE SERVICE CALLED 'TYPIKA'

The service of the Typika corresponds in a certain way to the Holy Liturgy, when this is not celebrated. At the Liturgy of saints who are commemorated, these are recited first. Initially, two psalms are sung: "Bless the Lord, my soul" [Ps 102], and "Praise the Lord, my soul" [Ps 145], since these contain praise of God and remind us of his boundless grace towards us, especially the graces deriving from the incarnation of the Word of God. Then the hymn of the incarnation is sung, i.e., "Only-begotten Word of God," etc.

CHAPTER 38. A SHORT EXPLANATION OF THE BEATITUDES OF THE SAVIOR

The Beatitudes of the Savior present him to us as the only blessed one, who, in fact, became poor for us, meek and lowly of heart, hungering and thirsting only for righteousness and executing it. They present to us the Lord, who only is merciful and forgiving, pure in heart, holy and undefiled, a peacemaker and king of peace; Son of God by nature, who was truly persecuted for righteousness' sake, despised, persecuted, unjustly reviled, surrendering on our behalf to the glory of his Father and our salvation; who alone possesses unbounded bliss and happiness.

Furthermore, these Beatitudes present and reveal to us as called blessed by the Savior himself those who imitate him, since they progress in virtue by stages. Becoming poor for Christ's sake they advance from poverty to gentleness. Since they show themselves to be impassive by their despisement of wealth, they hunger and thirst after righteousness; from righteousness they progress to mercy; from mercy to purity of heart; from purity to love and care for their neighbor and concern for his peace. Subsequently they advance to the more perfect love of God, and since they have great zeal for God's truth and righteousness are persecuted and suffer even greater and worse things, being envied for their piety and faith, persecuted, slandered, suffering everything for him, their rewarder and Savior. Thus also, when they suffer for

Christ they rejoice, and will rejoice and be glad then in the heavenly kingdom, for their reward is great in heaven.

These Beatitudes are recited as the teaching of the Savior and a presage of what is to come, or as a type of the Epistle and Gospel. Then we sing thrice the theological statement of of the Thief, i.e., his request to Christ on the Cross: "Remember me, Lord," etc. [Lk 23.42] by which request he enjoyed paradise, and assured by this in the Holy Trinity we also request paradise. Then the things said outside by all at the Liturgy are sung, and the angelic hymn, "Holy, Holy, Holy," three times. Then the Creed, the petition for forgiveness of all our sins, and finally the prayer given us by God, "Our Father," is recited, and the troparia appropriate for the day are added; then, "Lord, have mercy" forty times according to the order of the services, and there follow immediately the psalms of thanks to God for all his benefits, and especially for those relating to our nourishment: "I will bless the Lord" [Ps 33] and "I will exalt you, my God" [Ps 144]. After the Antidoron has been distributed for our sanctification, the Dismissal is performed.

CHAPTER 39. THREE SERVICES/SACRED FUNCTIONS BEGIN AT THE SANCTUARY AND END THERE: MATINS, THE HOLY LITURGY, AND VESPERS

The evening service is performed, like Matins, with extra splendor and care because—as we have said above—three times three services of praise are offered daily as confession and glorification to the Holy Trinity, which begin primarily at the sanctuary and should be ended there by a priest: Matins, the greatest sacred function of all, i.e., the Holy Liturgy, and Vespers. Every faithful person and every layperson should really attend these services of praise daily, and the other services as far as possible.

When the priest has given the blessing in the sanctuary, as though in heaven before God, somebody recites: "Come, let us worship . . ." thrice, thus inciting the others to understand and revere what is read. If it is an ordinary day, the whole of

the Introductory Psalm [Ps 103] is read, blessing the Lord
and recounting his creative work, thanking him for everything, for it is fitting always and especially at the close of day
to give thanks for everything. If it is a feast day it is read as far
as "Your hand is opened" [v. 28], and then the rest is sung
more festally by all, and at each verse we glorify the Holy
Trinity as creator of all. When the priest has said the Litany
of Peace and sung the Doxology, the others add psalms; if it
is an ordinary day, so as to complete the Psalter in a week; if
it is in Lent, it is recited twice for our greater labor and God's
glory, and for the propitiation of our sins.

CHAPTER 40. THE FIRST THREE PSALMS OF THE PSALTER REFER PRIMARILY TO THE LORD

If it is a feast day, after the Triadic Hymns and the Litany
are sung, the first three psalms referring primarily to the Lord
are read, since the Word of God became man and was by nature
the only blessed man who committed no sin, the tree of life
bearing fruit for us Christians who have believed in him. He
lives forever and does not wither, being passionless and immortal. Nor does he reject us, but saves us because we are his ever-
green leaves and fruit. He will scatter like dust the impious
and the demons, and he has conquered and put to shame the
kings and rulers who gathered against him. He was restored
as king of his church; as Son of God he received the inheritance of the nations, ruled over the ends of the earth, and is a
mighty shepherd. His oppressors, enviers and persecutors
multiplied, and finally delivered him to the death of the
cross. He was with his Father when he suffered in the flesh
passionless in his divinity, and revealed himself as our help
and our glory. Though he rested in the tomb, having died as
a human, yet as God he arose from sleep. This is why we say
"arise" and "save me, O God," for you have crushed all your
enemies, and "salvation is with the Lord and for his faithful
people" [Ps 3.9], i.e., for us, through the blessing of the cross.
After the psalms, when the priest has given thanks as is
customary and recited the Great Litany (i.e., the Litany of

Peace) and glorified the Holy Trinity, they sing, "Lord, I have cried . . ." [Ps 140] with its accompanying psalms, since they are compiled for the evening and offered as spiritual incense. Then physical incense is offered to God, starting from the sanctuary and filling all the nave, for God's glory and our sanctification, since then the divine grace of our glorified God is granted to us.

Having reached this point, it is appropriate for us to say what we can about the so-called "Litany of Peace," i.e., the Great and Lesser Litanies, as also about the Extended or Continuous Intercession, and the final petitions. Since these are recited by the priests and deacons at every service and at the Holy Liturgy, we should try to understand them as well as possible, and not take them for granted.

First, we will expound the so-called "Litany of Peace": "of peace" because the petitions request peace from God amongst ourselves — "litany" because we perform the petitions together or unitedly. When the priest has blessed God, since it is fitting to remember and preach him as the origin of all and provider of every good thing, he adds immediately: "In peace let us beseech the Lord." This shows our peace with God, since it is done with upright faith and conscience, and these are our peace with God. It shows our peace with all our brethren too, and our being free from angry thoughts towards anyone, "lifting holy hands" as Paul says [1 Tit 2.8], and as the Savior said: "When you pray, forgive what you have against anyone" [Mk 11.25], and similarly in another passage: "Peace I leave with you, peace to you . . ."[Jn 14.27]. For we need to have this in ourselves above all else, and to pray always with this peace, so at the outset we say: "In peace let us beseech the Lord," since the Savior himself recommends this in another passage, saying: "If you do not forgive others, neither will your Father forgive your transgressions" [Mt 6.15]. Because true peace is granted by God alone, because he is already at peace with us and his extreme mercy has effected our salvation, the priest adds: "For the peace from above and the salvation of our souls . . . " — since it is enough for God to look upon us with a sympathetic and peaceful eye and we enjoy salvation immediately. Then he requests general peace. "For the peace of the whole world . . .," since this is given by God and we are eager for it. Do you see how useful peace is? Because of it God also descended from heaven.

Then he continues: "For the good estate of the holy churches of God . . . ," aiming for peace in faith, and the good state and conduct of the Church. What follows has the same intention, since it petitions for the union of all, which should take place with upright faith, love and godly life.

Then he mentions the holy house and those entering it out of good order and zeal for the beauty of the holy house, to assemble in accord and piety, to offer to God of what we have received from the divine generosity.

Then he remembers the bishop, since he is the source of the priesthood and all Christianity. He remembers the priests as accessories of the holy services, the diaconate in Christ as serving at the mystery; all the clergy as assisting with the chanting and general order. He also remembers the people, as faithful and united with the clergy in belief and virtuous living, and as sanctified by these clerics. Do you see why it is called "Synapte" (Litany)? Because it gathers all into one, as the Savior prayed [Jn 10.21]. The kings, governors, and the army he joins with the people. However, since they are the protection of the populace and work for them, he remembers them separately as pious persons. Consider that in this Litany, in the secret prayers of the Liturgy, at the Diptychs and in the final "Prayer behind the Ambo," the Church mentions first the bishops and priest and all the clergy, and then adds the kings. This by divine decree and commanded from heaven, for he that transmits sanctification as a cleric is superior to those sanctified, even if they are kings: "For the lesser is blessed by the greater" [Rom 7.7]. I do not understand how this order has been changed altogether in some places, so that often the clergy appear in a lower rank than the laity, and without being of lower rank are given orders here and in many other respects because of the disdain of some laics towards divine matters. So the Church prays, keeping the law of Paul precisely in praying for kings and those of high rank, especially those that are Orthodox, that God may assist them in their wars and defeat all their enemies, so that we, too, may live a quiet and peaceful life and maintain the things of piety in modesty and order.

Since we have need of protection, and the rulers of protecting us, we pray for the city that protects us and — moved by Christian charity — for all other cities also. Furthermore, for all countries, since not only the cities are inhabited, but villages and towns are also. Since the whole aim of the cities is to preserve themselves for their inhabitants, we add: ". . . for those dwelling in faith in them . . ."; for those in faith, because we should not pray for the impious. Since we also have need of the things that sustain our bodies, since they and ourselves are of God, we add: "For temperate weather . . . ," for the health of our bodies; ". . . for abundance of the fruits of the earth . . . ," for what is needed to nourish us; "and for peaceful times . . . ," since they preserve our life and style of living, whereas tumults and abnormal times are the cause of affliction and destruction.

Since the experiences of mankind are many and its needs various, and since life and style of living differ with the rank and circumstances of each person, the Church prays for all together. "For those travelling by ship"—for those on the sea; "for travelers by land"—for those journeying on dry land; "for the sick" — for any illness whatever; "for those working and laboring, and prisoners in need and danger," gathering all into one the Church prays for their salvation. Do you see that the Church imitates God in thinking of everyone? That is, it gathers all and prays for that which is why this prayer is called "Synapte" [Litany]. Then, after it has called and incited all to pray for general salvation, and ordered them to invoke God for each other in accordance with the apostolic command, it turns and addresses itself to God who can save all, saying: "Assist. . ." — for you alone are the assistance of us who are weak and perishing; ". . . save . . ." — for you alone are the Savior of the endangered and despairing; ". . ." have mercy . . ." — for you see nothing worthy in us and must have mercy because you are by nature merciful; " . . . preserve . . ." — for many are those who scheme against

us and oppress us, and you alone our God can protect us by
your grace— not because of our works and petitions, since we
are polluted by sin and our works are unclean, but by your
grace alone. The incarnation of your only-begotten Son our
Savior is an outstanding gift, which is also called grace.

So, propitiating God towards us in this way the priest (or
the deacon, if there is one) recites the Litany of Peace.
Through these petitions and the secret prayers within, the
priest exhorts and incites us to commend or offer ourselves
to God, both ourselves and one another and our whole life.
Consider the salutory and marvelous nature of the prayer:
"Remembering our most-holy and immaculate Lady . . ." —
which repeats the praises of the all-glorified Theotokos as far
as possible";. . . with all the saints . . ." — here the prayer puts
forward the leader of the saints, the means of sanctification,
the divine instrument through which we have been saved,
together with all those sanctified through her. We invoke
them to help us, since they too were of the same nature,
taking thought for us and having power with God because
they struggled for his glorification; and we commemorate
them, i.e., remember them because they always remember us
for our salvation; He says "ourselves" because we owe ourselves to God; "each other" because we have been commanded
to love one another; "our whole life" because this was given
to us by God, and in a certain sense we should offer to Christ
our God all our thoughts and deeds in this life, our actions,
our souls and bodies, because he instructs us to dedicate
ourselves as a living sacrifice to himself, who was sacrificed
for us and gave himself for our redemption.

We should, therefore, place our trust in him who offered
his life for us and gave himself as our heavenly food, who
provides for us and loves us, is always concerned to save us,
for he is our Savior—without him nothing can live or think
or do anything. Nor can our perverse adversary snatch from
the hand of the Father those who have dedicated themselves
to Christ, for Christ is the hand of God, his arm and the Holy
Spirit. See then, those with understanding find the contents
of this prayer very good, more perfect than all the others.

This is why to the other petitions those present say only "Lord, have mercy," invoking the divine mercy, while here they say: "To you, Lord," i.e., to you, Christ our God, we dedicate and offer ourselves.

This dedication is essential as we rightly confess, since it is the confession which dedicates to God our upright faith and the offering of ourselves; it unites us with God, attracts his help, unites us with the most holy Mother of the Divine Word, and activates her intercession for us. It is also essential to do this always with works— meaning correct belief, Christian life in purity, truth and justice, and for us to occupy ourselves with these prayers, since being dedicated to God through the confession, sanctified by his sacraments, and otherwise delivered over to Christ, as ransomed from death by him, we ought not to do anything except the things of Christ.

Regarding this dedication, this offering, all the saints remind us and so does Christ himself, who indeed set us an example at the time of his passion, for then he dedicated us to the Father: "Keep them in your name" [Jn 17.17] and "sanctify them in your truth" [Jn 17.17] etc.— he being the truth.

Having completed these things, the priest adds the glorification of the Holy Trinity saying: "For to you is due . . ." through this theology and doxology affirming what was said before and witnessing that these things will be given us by God. The psalm verses recited with troparia or idiomela are on Sundays to the number of ten, because this is a perfect number; on feasts of saints eight are said, for the eighth and eternal day in which all the godly will be with Christ, as they are now in spirit; on ordinary days they are restricted to the number of six, since the saints became higher than perception, which is pentadic— and since six is twice the Holy Trinity. These hymns are sung by both choirs, and refer either to the resurrection or to some other feast or saint in question. At the last verse the choirs come together, showing the accord and unity of the whole world through the Savior. Together they bow before the sanctuary and cry: "For His mercy

remained with us . . ." [Ps 116.2] signifying by this the unity
of the Gentiles through the grace of Christ, and that through
his loving kindness he suffered for our sake, established his
power by the cross, conquered the Devil, and united us with
himself. Again, together they sing "Glory . . ." and "Now
and ever . . . ," ceaselessly glorifying the indivisible Holy
Trinity. Then they glorify the Virgin Mother of God at the
end, by confessing the incarnation of him who took flesh of
her, and because of her great and powerful intercession.

CHAPTER 41. THE SIGNIFICANCE OF THE ENTRANCE AT VESPERS, AND THE PRIEST'S BOWING, RISING, AND GOING UP INTO THE SANCTUARY

Then the priest performs the Entrance, coming out bare-
headed from the sanctuary with censer and incense, and in
the center of the church bowing his head and praying, raising
his head, signing with his hand and the censer, and reentering
the sanctuary. What does this signify? That the only-begotten
Son of God, after descending to us from the heavenly apse,
i.e., from the spheres, was taken up into heaven again, taking
us with him also. Thus by his exit from the sanctuary, the bowing of his head, rising and signing aloud: "Wisdom, be upstanding," signing with the censer and raising the Gospel (if there
is an Entrance with the Gospel), and returning again to the
sanctuary— by all this the mystery of God's dispensation is
symbolized.

Again, the exit of the priest from the sanctuary and his
descent to the center of the nave signifies the descent of
Christ from heaven and his humility. That the priest wears
sacerdotal vestments signifies the incarnation; that he stands
in the center and bows his head signifies that the Savior was
crucified for us and died at the center of the earth, and descended to Hades. This is why the priest prays in silence with
bowed head then, because the God-Man offered himself to
the heavenly Father, and descending into Hades redeemed us
from the tyranny of Hades. For this reason also the priest
offers incense, which is by nature very fragrant (symbolizing

the holy soul and life of our Savior) or holds the Gospel, because the Lord condescended to us humans; and by raising his head the priest signifies the resurrection of Christ, and that through this he raised us with him. He proclaims and shows this— either by making the sign of the cross with the censer and chanting "Wisdom, be upstanding," or by elevating the Gospel — while this coming up and entering the sanctuary signifies his holy ascension from the earth; that he returned to where he was in heaven, i.e., with that body which he wore for our sake and offered as a sacrifice for us; and that thus he raised and sanctified us also.

These then are all the significations of the Entrance, and it is necessary for us to study them always and keep them in mind, for through the descent of God from heaven we received our salvation.

CHAPTER 42. WHY THE ENTRANCE IS PERFORMED MORE SOLEMNLY ON SATURDAY EVENINGS AND ON OTHER FEASTS OF OUR LORD AND THE SAINTS

The Vespers Entrance signifies — among other things— that the condescension of God took place at the end of the ages. This is why the Entrance is performed more solemnly on Saturdays, since on this Sabbath day the descent of our Savior into Hades and his resurrection took place. On the feasts of our Lord it is also performed solemnly, because he who descended from heaven performed the mystery celebrated on that day, and at the commemorations of saints because his ascent into heaven transported those saints, too, with their souls and received them with him, and will receive them with their bodies so as to have them fully with him always.

CHAPTER 43. SIGNIFICANCE OF THE ENTRANCE AT MATINS

In the Great Church the Matins Entrance also signifies what we said above, especially that Christ descended into Hades with his soul and rose with his body, and his resurrection was announced by the angels. This is why at Matins the priest proclaims the resurrection from the ambo — like a second angel on the stone, or rather as an angel.

CHAPTER 44. ON SUNDAYS THE MATINS ENTRANCE IS PERFORMED IN THE MONASTERIES ALSO, AS A TYPE OF THE RESURRECTION

This Matins Entrance takes places in the monasteries also before the singing of the Kanons, when the so-called Matins (Dawn) Gospel is read, since this teaches what occurred at the resurrection of the Lord as seen on that day. It is performed thus:— The priest comes out of the awesome sanctuary like Christ coming out of the tomb, holding the Gospel like an angel and thus symbolizing Christ whom he preaches. All come to revere— like the disciples and the women bearing myrrh— and kiss the Gospel while the appropriate hymn is sung: "Having seen the resurrection of Christ . . ."

These things are done at Matins, but since we are discussing the Entrance it seems not inappropriate to discuss this also. When the Vespers Entrance has been completed and they are chanting the holy hymn "Gladdening light . . ." [Phos Hilaron] (which is ancient and fitting for evening at the Entrance because it proclaims the Holy Trinity and the incarnation of the Divine Word, and is said to be a creation of the holy martyr Athenogenes) the deacon chants "Wisdom . . ." and the seated bishop gives the peace, as Christ before and after his resurrection gave it to us, and having ascended into heaven leads us there eternally.

CHAPTER 45. THE SIGNIFICANCE OF THE PROKEIMENA SUNG EACH DAY

Then the Evening Prokeimenon is sung solemnly. This Prokeimenon is the prophecy of the feast and a psalm-verse teaching us about that day.

On Saturday evening it witnesses to the resurrection, which is why we sing "The Lord has reigned . . ." [Ps 92], because the Risen One has conquered and ruled over Death; "He has put on beauty," i.e., the incorruption of our nature, which before him was corruptible, and by rising again, he established the world that believed in him.

On Sunday evenings we sing: "Behold, bless the Lord . . ." [Ps 133], because of the angels who bless him unceasingly, and for the souls of his servants.

On Monday evenings: "The Lord will hear me when I cry to him" [Ps 4.4], for those of the faithful who call to Him in penitence, and for the Forerunner, the preacher of penitence.

On Tuesday evenings, for the assistance of the Savior's passion and his mercy to us in the cross: "Your mercy, O Lord, will follow me all the days of my life" [Ps 22.6].

On Wednesday evenings that of the apostles is sung: "O God, save me in your name . . ." [Ps 53.1], since through his apostles we are saved in the name of the Lord, as they preached the Lord to us, showing themselves to be divine preachers, and saved us with the cooperation of God, who confirms the word as it is written in the Gospels.

On Thursday evenings we praise the great assistance of the cross: "My help is in the Lord, who has made heaven and earth" [Ps 120.2], for he who created heaven and earth assisted us by being crucified in the flesh.

On Friday evenings: "God is my helper . . ." [Ps 58.11], because of the multitude of saints who co-operate with our Savior for our assistance, and for the souls of the faithful departed, since God became help and assistance to the saints and mercy to the dead, granting them salvation.

On feast days, instead of the Prokeimenon we sing: "Alleluia" which is a Hebrew word meaning "praise the Lord," "indwelling of God" and "The Lord comes" — preaching his first and second comings. It also prophesies the things relating to his passion and resurrection, i.e., as the Lord came into the world to suffer for our sake and be resurrected, so he will come again at the end of days to judge the whole earth. Thus being always concerned and remembering our sins, let us — as awaiting the Lord — cleanse ourselves from every stain, and not be over eager to celebrate splendidly, but let us cry to God in mourning and grief, and let us praise and invoke him always, awaiting his coming at the last day. Prokeimena are sung as preludes to the feasts and the ensuing days.

CHAPTER 46. THE EXTENDED LITANY AND THE PETITIONS, WHICH ARE MOST NECESSARY

After this the Extended Litany and the Petitions are performed by the priest — the Extended Litany for mercy on everyone, faithful kings and the local bishop; for the superior of the monastery, those having the care of the holy church, for the Orthodox present and for all the faithful everywhere. The Petitions request that we may pass the evening and night (or the day, as we say at Matins) wholly sinless and peaceful; that we may have the angel of peace, protector of our souls and bodies, that we may find forgiveness of our sins; that we may be given what is best and useful for us by the divine mercy, and peace for the world; that we may pass the rest of our lives in penitence and peace, as befits Christians; that the end of our lives may be faithful, holy and peaceful; and that we may find a good defence on the fearful day of the second coming. Then, for the intercession of the Theotokos who has power in all matters; and of all the saints, since they too have freedom of access and power with God because of their pains and martyrdoms suffered in living for Christ. They incite us to offer "ourselves" to our Christ and God, since we owe ourselves to God as his creatures; and "one another" because we ought to assist our neighbors also according to the commandment: "Love God, and your neighbor as yourself" [Lk 10.27] ; and finally "our whole life" given by God. We perform this offering immediately, chanting the words: "To you, Lord," i.e., we commend ourselves into your hands.

However, it is essential that we perform this offering by works, since whoever offers himself ought to be in the power of him to whom he is offered, so as to attract the protection of the latter and to enjoy his concern and care. You see then that these petitions request great benefits of God for us, which they produce in those who understand them. This is why we see in the Church some pious men who are ecstatic almost during these petitions and implore with their whole soul and really offer themselves to God. We also see others who do not feel what is being said through spiritual perception.

After this, the priest glorifies God aloud and prays for peace upon all, chanting: "Let us bow our heads . . ." as a sign of servanthood and petition. Firstly, he bows his head, confessing himself to be a humble servant, and prays for the priests— because even he does not have confidence in himself, since he also is in need of mercy. For this reason he prays in piety and silence, in fear and trembling, while he speaks and intercedes with God, saying: "O Lord God, who bows the heavens and descends for the salvation of mankind. We do not proffer or offer of our own things, for they are all unworthy of the Lord and unclean, but the work of your love and humility. Look down, Lord, upon your inheritance, for they have not bowed their heads to men, but to you, seeking salvation from you. Protect them in soul and body at all times and today from every adversary, spiritual or corporeal. Then, as if having confidence that he will receive what is requested, he raises his head and glorifies God aloud: "Blessed be the power of your kingdom . . . ," etc., as if to say: you alone are king, glorified, blessed, and all-powerful. Then the Lite follows at once.

CHAPTER 47. THE LITE IN THE NARTHEX, AND THE OTHER PROCESSIONS OUTSIDE THE NAVE

This Lite takes place in the narthex on Saturdays and feasts. In time of some divine visitation or other disaster or common misfortune, more gather together and perform this through or outside the city or around its walls. This procession is an intercession to God and a general petition, and takes place either as propitiation for some act of God's wrath, or as thanks to God for the benefits granted to us by his grace. That we come outside the holy nave signifies the expulsion from paradise because of the transgression of Adam, and that through this, paradise and heaven were closed to us. That we pass to the center of the city and chant mournfully signifies that by our sins we have polluted and profaned the city and everything in it. That we go outside the city shows that we humble ourselves and judge ourselves unworthy to cry and petition God from inside the city which we have polluted by inhabiting it. As we fell away from the paradise of our sacred homeland by the transgression of our forefathers, so similarly in this city where we were born—or rather reborn through baptism— and where we were made worthy of so many good things by God, being deceived by the serpent we were foolishly corrupted and became abominations, polluting the holy place with our impurity, and being driven into waste and barren places by the visitation of God, and as impious we dwell in them.

When the Lite is performed on Saturdays or certain feasts it takes place in the narthex, since our Savior descended to our depths so that we might propitiate him, and before the gates of the holy temple— as if before the heavenly gates— we implore God. For we are not worthy to lift up our eyes and look up to the height of heaven unless we repent and cry: "We have sinned." Then he comes from heaven and responds to those who are repentant and afflicted of heart, he embraces us mercifully and receives us. This petition of the priest before the doors of the nave signifies that he implores and beseeches God to open to us Eden and heaven, and for the mercy of God in particular, which we have closed against us by our sins.

So, while we stand outside chanting the customary verses, the priest offers the customary prayers for all the people and God's inheritance, requesting that he may exalt the horn of the Christians, saying: "O Lord, save your people and bless your inheritance . . ." When they have sung "Lord, have mercy" as a general prayer, the priest again prays to God for the kings, since they head the ranks of the faithful and strive for the faith. He also prays for the local bishop, our spiritual father, for every Christian soul, for the peace of the churches — that the enemy may not sow tares of heresy there, for the faithful departed, for the freeing of captives, for the recovery and health of the sick, for those who labor in Christ, and for all the brethren. Then that penitential and powerful petition is said: "Lord, have mercy," many times in succession, and finally again thrice to the glory of the Holy Trinity, because this petition is offered to the same Holy Trinity.

CHAPTER 48. THE FINAL PRAYERS OF THE LITE

In this prayer the priest beseeches our good and loving God to hear us all and to be merciful to us all, and benevolently grant his mercy to us all. Then he tells us to bow in humility and incline our heads before God in a gesture of servanthood, and turning towards the west he prays over us who have bowed our heads, as on the part of God, for all good things, invoking our most merciful master and God. As mediation he advances first the intercessions of theTheotokos and then those of the angels and apostles, martyrs, hierarchs, venerable monastics, and all the saints together. He prays through their intercession and not through us unworthy and sinful people, imploring God that our prayer may be acceptable, and that we may be granted remission of our sins; that we may remain under the protection of his wings; that our enemies — whether spiritual or corporeal — may be kept far from us; that our lives may be peaceful; and finally for mercy for the world and for us from him, the loving and gracious Master, who through his goodness became man and alone is merciful.

CHAPTER 49. WHY LIGHTS ARE ALWAYS CARRIED IN FRONT

Having completed this, the priest enters the nave through the royal gate as though entering heaven, and preceded by lights as when he came out, and as occurs at each Entrance as a type and copy of the divine light and the saints, and especially of the unoriginate Father. The others follow and enter, with the presiding cleric leading and preceding, typifying Jesus Christ. When the choirs on both sides have combined in psalmody and all are standing in the center— as though heaven had been opened to us and the angels had been united with us mortals through Christ — the Aposticha are sung with verses appropriate to the feast being celebrated.

If it is Sunday, they sing verses of the Resurrection to "The Lord has reigned . . ." [Ps 92]. If it is some other feast, the appropriate verses and idiomela are sung. If it is the festival of some saint, whether hierarch or martyr or monastic, they sing the psalm verses belonging to its stichera. They are called stichera because they are sung outside at the Lite without versicles, and which are therefore called Aposticha. Then "Glory . . ." and "Now and ever . . ." are sung with their idiomela— the former from those of the feast or one of the saints; the latter for the Theotokos, because of her powerful intercessin for us. Then at once: Now dismiss . . ." [Nunc dimittis] is said reverently by somebody, being the canticle of Symeon who received the Lord. In this prayer he requests release of the soul from the flesh, since he had seen the salvation of God. We seek release or freedom of the soul from the passions, from the temptations of the enemy, and from the twofold illnesses of the body and soul. It is not surprising that we ask to be granted release of the body and peace and salvation, whenever it is his sacred will. This "Now dismiss . . ." presages the completion of the aim of our hymns — that he may grant us the light of grace, salvation, and glory.

After this the prayer of the Trisagion and "Our Father" is added like a holy seal, and when the priest has glorified the kingdom of God, we sing the Troparion of the feast: "O Virgin Theotokos, hail most-favored Mary . . ."loudly and melodically. This was the message of the archangel at the holy conception of the Virgin Mother of God.

Since this message is the beginning of the dispensation of salvation, and since it is logical that it occurs on Sunday like the resurrection, it is therefore recited at the vigils of Sundays and feasts of saints (except those of our Lord) since the Mother of God is the leader and sanctity of all the saints because of her virgin birth giving, i.e., of our master Christ, the Savior of the world.

CHAPTER 50. THE ARTOKLASIA (BREAKING OF BREAD)

Then another sacred ceremony is performed, handed down from above by our Savior. Five loaves are set out on a table, and in an appropriate vessel wheat, wine, and oil. The priest censes around them as a type of the cross while "O Virgin Theotokos . . ." is being sung — not because they are holy but because they will be sanctified, or rather as being presanctified through the cross and the incense. So he does not bow his head while censing, but stands with head high in imitation of the Savior he represents, and involving him he takes up one of the five loaves. When the deacon has said: "Let us beseech the Lord," the priest chants: "O Lord Jesus Christ our God, who blessed the five loaves and satisfied five thousand with them, bless these loaves also . . . ," and while saying this he makes the sign of the cross with one of the loaves over the other four, signifying that Christ did this— although he took the five loaves into his hands. Replacing the loaf, he blessed them crosswise with his hand, witnessing that Christ blesses them, and also includes the wheat, wine, and oil in the blessing: ". . . and increase them in this holy monastery and in your world always," for he fills every living thing with goodness when he opens his hand, as it is written [Ps 103.28]. Then the priest recites the appropriate doxology: "For it is you who bless and sanctify all things . . . ," praising the bread of life, i.e., the Son, with the Father and the Holy Spirit. Then all recite the thanksgiving which Job once expressed to God: "Blessed be the name of the Lord. . ." [Job 1.21] and "I will bless the Lord . . ."[Ps 33], since this is the most fitting psalm, recited by David for the remission of our debts. The priest signs us all and invokes God's blessing upon us all, since this is the true food and drink — nourishment does not commend us to God, according to Paul [1 Cor 8.8], and God alone is the giver of every good thing. The priest leaves without performing the Dismissal, since Matins is joined on after the Reading has been performed. The loaves and the wine, sanctified by the blessing of the priest, are distributed among those present, and are for those who receive them in faith purveyors of grace, healing and many other gifts.

These things are done if there is a Vigil (Agrypnia). If there is not, after the bowing of the heads no Lite takes place nor any blessing of loaves, but the Aposticha are sung plus "Now dismiss . . ." with the Trisagion and Dismissal. However, certain zealots, even when there is no Vigil— as happens because of illness or paucity of monks, perhaps — perform the Lite of Vespers, then the Aposticha and Dismissal at once. They do not bless the loaves, because this was ordained primarily because of the fatigue of the Vigil, so that the Christians could enjoy the blessing of Christ and some consolation for their fatigue, and also prepare themselves by prayer and care for Communion of the awesome mysteries, especially the clergy.

Behold, the exposition has also been completed. Let us now discuss Compline, about which we will say briefly what is most necessary.

Cleric: Fulfill your reward in this respect also, holy master, so that this teaching may be complete in all regards for us.

CHAPTER 51. THE SERVICE OF COMPLINE (APODEIPNON)

Archbishop: As we said above, in the large monasteries Compline is recited together with Vespers, as a common prayer before the gates of the nave, but in the cenobia and among monks, secular priests, and pious laics it is sung after the evening meal. During Great Lent — both in the large monasteries and everywhere — it is sung separately after Vespers and the meal, which takes place once a day only. Compline of Great Lent, which is called "Great Compline," is divided into three sections as a type of the Holy Trinity and for the propitiation of our sins. Since the Typika describe it, there is no need for us to add a detailed exposition, especially since we have already explained almost all the prayers and since the psalms and prayers of Compline are penitential and confessional, seeking forgiveness and propitiation, and for us to pass the night unmolested and unpolluted by satanic fantasies, and to arise with zeal and eagerness at the time of the Midnight Office and Matins.

The so-called "Small Compline" is termed so because it is briefer and one service, not divided into three sections like the other. It is recited daily, and its psalms are the same as the main ones of Great Compline. They are three as a type of the Holy Trinity. The most holy Creed is also recited as a confession of piety, and "It is worthy . . ." because of the incarnation of the Divine Word and the intercession of the Mother of God. In accordance with the patristic tradition, after the Creed we invoke the Mother of God and the angels and saints to intercede with God for us, as we invoke them in the Great Church, since it is essential in many respects to invoke those intercessors and helpers who are closer to God and have freedom of access and power.

After that the prayer of the Trisagion is recited, being the start, middle, and end of all services, plus "Lord, have mercy" forty times, for the sanctification of the hours and days of our life. Then the prayer to the Theotokos: "Immaculate, undefiled, most-favored . . ." recited for all the benefits — whether present, at the end of our lives, for the future and heavenly life — as also according to custom the invocation of the Mother of God as more honored than the Cherubim takes place so that she may keep and protect us under the shadow of her wings. The usual prayer is added by the priest: "May God have pity on us . . . ," then the final prayer: "Grant us, Master, who are going to sleep . . ." Small Compline is also ended in another way which is more appropriate and usual today; after "Lord, have mercy," they recite "You who at every season . . . ," "More honored than the Cherubim . . . ," "May God have pity on us . . . ," and then the prayer to the Theotokos: "Immaculate, undefiled . . . ," etc., plus "And grant us, Master . . . " This is customary everywhere and is described in the Typika.

CHAPTER 52. THE GENERAL NORMS SHOULD BE MAINTAINED

Certain people out of zeal sing the Offices in an individual way, not in public but privately, for we must maintain the common norms for good order and to avoid strife and scandal. Such persons may be given permission to hold services in their cells — alone or with certain disciples or brethren of like mind — with the agreement and counsel of the fathers. You know that out of penitence Kanons are sung with Compline in the evenings, as also the Great Kanon and the Kanons of the Theotokos, and the Service of the Akathist every Friday evening — both in the holy monasteries and by many others.

Everyone who is zealous in this regard and labors will have a greater reward in proportion to his labors, but one lot is offered by the choice and zeal of individuals, while the other is laid down publicly and openly, and should not be contravened except for illness or great necessity. However, for the sick mental prayer is most beneficial and necessary, but for those in tribulation, grief or need, public prayer and recourse to God is more useful and beneficial. For who beside God can save us from afflictions, and vain is every hope in mankind: "We will perform mighty deeds in God" [Ps 59.12], "He cries to me and I will hear him" [Ps 90.15], and many similar things said by David.

There are some who do not perform what is prescribed, but many things of their own. Having their souls always united with God they mortify the body with fasting and prostration, and will be set among the ranks of the martyrs; and it is fitting that we imitate them as far as possible, so as to be numbered with them in their ranks through little labor and pain, through the extreme graciousness of God. If we are unable to do everything like them, let us at least imitate them in part, for if we have the zeal God will strengthen us through this zeal so that we will imitate them completely — as he strengthened them also. Through this small and slight contribution, God will have mercy on us because of our weakness and will make us worthy to be set with them in heaven, since our Master is so loving towards mankind and so merciful, needing only a small token from us; then he generously fulfills all and saves us, and sets us in the company of his saints.

The contents of the Jerusalem Typikon also give details.

CHAPTER 53. THE ORDINANCES AND PRESCRIPTIONS OF
THE CHURCH AND THE SERVICE CALLED 'ASMATIC'

We shall see symbolized very clearly the details of the dispensation of Christ in the service appropriately called "Asmatic" which was handed down to us from above by the holy
Fathers, as we said. This melodic service was originally sung
by all the catholic churches of the entire world, which recited
nothing without melody (except the priest's prayers and the
deacon's litanies) — especially the Great Churches such as
Constantinople, Antioch, and Thessalonike, where alone
today it is performed in the Church of the Holy Wisdom. It is
performed in the following way, as we expound.

CHAPTER 54. ASMATIC VESPERS

At Asmatic Vespers it was formerly usual for the acolytes
to fill the whole church with incense before the service, to
the glory of God and as a type of his sacred glory, which
once filled the tabernacle so that Moses and Aaron could not
enter until it rose. Again, this was done in imitation of the
Temple of Solomon, which was filled with the glory of God,
so that the priests could not stand and celebrate before the
Lord until the cloud became invisible and dissolved. This
order of censing is kept at Matins similarly.

CHAPTER 55. THE SIGNIFICANCE OF THE SILENT CENSING
BEFORE VESPERS AND MATINS

Nowadays this is not done except at the time of the Liturgy, and the deacon or priest only censes the sanctuary—or
the whole church—silently after the Proskomide [service of
preparation] as a type of that divine glory. However, in some
monasteries this is still done before Great Vespers, signifying
the divine glory and the grace given to the priest by an angel,
and that the house of the Lord is full of glory.

At Asmatic Vespers the priest, standing before the Holy
Table as though before the throne of God in heaven, blesses

God in Trinity saying: "Blessed be our God. . . ,"for this is not customary in the order of the chant and is from the Old Testament only while that which he says at the Holy Liturgy is "Blessed be the kingdom of the Father and of the Son and of the Holy Spirit." In this fashion he theologizes the unity of the divine kingdom and nature, and the triadic character of God, i.e., the preaching of grace and the knowledge and confession of the one God in Trinity.

Then he recites the Litany of Peace, first giving us peace as from God and teaching us all to request this peace. However, we should realize that all these arrangements have been altered — only that of the Liturgy remains and is done according to the old rite. Having blessed God in this way, the priest says the Litany of Peace, and the three Antiphons are sung as type of the Holy Trinity, being taken from the old sung service. Being ignorant of this, some people regard and call Asmatic Verspers "Liturgy" when the three Antiphons and Trisagion are sung at it. Those who had this service from the start, i.e., the Constantinopolitans, now admire it more, as also the service and order of the Trithekte (Third & Sixth Hour) during the fasts, and also the so-called Pannychis, which then used to take place every evening— especially during Great Lent, during the first week and Holy Week—because the prayers prescribed for the Pannychis are essential, and the details of the Trithekte from ancient tradition. The latter are part of the Hours, but are also called by the name of the Holy Liturgy, as we shall soon discuss briefly.

Now let us continue with Asmatic Vespers. When the priest has given the blessing and recited all the petitions for peace and "Assist, save, have mercy . . . ," the cantors sing: "And hear me: Glory be to you, O God." This sung versicle is necessary, and is taken from the psalm" Incline your ear, Lord, and hear me" [Ps 85]. The next one is taken from the angels: "Glory to God in the heights" and "Heaven and earth are full of his glory" and Blessed be the glory of the Lord." Then the priest chants: "Remembering our most holy Lady..."and loudly praises God in Trinity, saying: "For to you is due glory, honor and worship . . ." Thus each of the psalms is recited together with "Glory be to you, O God." "Hear me..."

is recited because — as we said above — it belongs with the following psalm, and it is customary at the other services also to prefix a part of the verse of the following psalm always, preluding it either by "Alleluia" or "Glory to you" or some refrain (*hypopsalma*). This is called *hypopsalma* because it is sung together with the psalm by verses — first the verse is said, then this, e.g., "Incline your ear, O Lord, and hear me" — "Glory be to you, O God," and so on.

Always at Vespers is sung "O Lord, incline your ear" because our Savior and Master, the sun of righteousness, inclined the heavens and came down, remaining unapproachable, and because the physical sun inclines towards its setting at evening, and through all this (inclining, setting, rising) it proclaims the unsetting and splendid Sun of Righteousness who appeared in the flesh, and again it symbolizes the sojourning of the Divine Word, and that God illumined the day of his first coming, descended under the earth into Hades, rose again and ascended into heaven, bringing about for us the unending day and illumining the whole world.

This is why the whole psalm "Incline your ear, O Lord," is recited by verses by both choirs, with "Glory be to you, O God," to each verse. It is clear from the prayers that the custom of this service is ancient, since the first prayer of the so-called Lychnika (Lamp-lighting Prayers) contains the whole sense and the words from the psalms. Similarly you will find in the other prayers that they have a sense appropriate to the psalms and antiphons, and words taken from these psalms — as also the Prayer of the Vespers Entrance, "At evening, morning, and midday . . . ," since it is to "Lord, I have cried" and to the verses of this that the Entrance is performed and the prayer is recited. It also contains ideas and words from the psalms sung, so as to offer all to God in the prayer: "Let my prayer arise as incense before you" [Ps 140.2] ; "Do not incline our hearts to evil words" [Ps 140.4] and "For on you, O Lord, my eyes . . ." [v. 8] — for at this verse the priest is invited to exit from the sanctuary. This shows, I think, the petition and prophecy concerning the indwelling and incarnation of the Lord, our salvation from Hades and destruction, through his passion and resurrection. So the first of the can-

tors calls the priest in the words of David: "O Lord, incline
the heavens and come down" [Ps 143.5] and "Send out
your power" [v.7] and "Come to save us" and as though
from Hades he chants: "For on you, Lord, my eyes are fixed, in you I have hoped: do not take away my soul"[Ps 140.8].
So also the priest comes out at this verse, signifying the descent of Christ to us and into Hades, and his resurrection by
which we are redeemed from Hades, and his ascent again
into heaven.

During the early centuries, the Psalter was recited in the
evening as it is now at Matins, and the monasteries imitated
this arrangement to some extent by always reciting one Kathisma (section) of the Psalter at Vespers and two at Matins.
Nowadays, because of weakness or carelessness, an antiphon
of the Psalter is no longer read at Vespers, except during Great
Lent and on Saturday evenings, and this only in the [Church
of the] Holy Wisdom in Thessalonike, where— since slothful
and careless persons grumbled— we have ordered that only
one psalm should be recited: "Blessed is the man" [Ps 1] to a
melody in the Mode. During Great Lent the six Antiphons
are to be recited in order, or one Kathisma only. The psalm
"Incline" contains both petition and glorification of God; it
praises and glorifies the Lord who suffered for us, Jesus Christ,
calling him merciful, gracious, and faithful, and prays that we
may be given a sign for good, i.e., the Cross on which the
Savior was nailed in the flesh and towards evening gave up his
divine spirit, and it requests that we be given power and salvation. The "Glory be . . . " is sung, and the other choir sings,
"Now and forever . . . ," with "Glory to you, O God . . ."

Then the priest again recites the Small Litany: "Again and
again . . . ," and the cantor sings melodically "The inhabited
world, Alleluia." When the priest has said: "Assist, save . . . ,"
the cantor adds: "Your universe, O God, do you assist, save
and have mercy upon us by your manifestation." For this is
what the Alleluia means, since this Hebrew word is interpreted
as "the sojourning of God," "the coming and manifestation of
God," and is the hymn par excellence of the mystery of the
divine dispensation, which is why we say it continually. It is
also sung before the Gospel, since it manifest the coming of

Christ, saying "God comes, who also has come and will come again from heaven."

When the priest has chanted: "Remembering our most blessed Lady . . ." and commended us all to God through the prayers of the saints, he sings aloud: "For yours is the power," glorifying the one God in Trinity; and immediately the cantor sings the Prokeimenon of the day, also called the final antiphon. Another antiphon used to be recited, but is now omitted.

On Saturday evenings we say: "Let God arise. . ." [Ps 67], and "Glory be . . ." and "Now and ever . . ." joined to "Lord, I have cried . . ." and the hypopsalma. On Sundays is said: "Your life-giving resurrection we glorify, O Lord . . ." on one Sunday, and "Your saving resurrection we glorify, O Lord . . ." on the other. While the following verses are sung in this way, the priest makes the Entrance — or many priests and deacons with him according to the order — preceded by lights and with censer and incense, as a type of the order above and of the transmission of God's grace from the sanctuary, and also as typifying that we extend our prayer into heaven like fragrant and pure incense—as the psalm and prayer recited at this time says, and also the prayer recited with bowed head by the priest: "At evening and morning and midday . . .," which matches what is sung. It says: "Direct our prayer as incense before you," "Do not incline our hearts to evil words," "Save us from all those who hunt our souls," "To you, Lord, Lord, our eyes are directed," and "Do not put us to shame, our God" — and then the priestly doxology follows.

When the priests have lifted their heads, the sign of the cross is made and "Blessed be the entrance of your saints" is said, and: "Wisdom, be upstanding," with the sign of the cross made with the censer. All this signifies the descent of our Savior at the end of the days and the sunset of this life, his life sanctified like incense, the offering of ourselves to God the Father through the most holy body in Holy Communion. He set us an example by being humiliated to the cross and death, descended into Hades, and arose, conquering Hades by the Cross, and ascended into the Holy of Holies, heaven, to prepare for our entry there also.

For this reason the cantor, at the verse: "For to you, Lord ..." turns to the west and making a reverence calls to the priest, who represents the Lord, saying: "For to you, Lord ..." This shows our hope in the Lord, our being freed and saved through our Lord, as we said above. Then the priest goes up to the sanctuary and enters, as the Savior did, into heaven.

The hymns of the resurrection are sung on the ambon in imitation of the angels who hymn the resurrection of the Savior, and of the apostles who proclaim him to the world. While these are being sung, the priest or deacon censes, since the grace of the all-holy Spirit was sent upon us by the risen and ascended Christ. After "Glory be" and "Now and ever ..." the Prokeimenon is sung, that "the Lord has reigned" — conquering the Devil and all his demons, and "has put on beauty" — the immortality and incorruption of the flesh (as we explained above) and "has established the world" by faith.

Then the Extended Litany is performed at once by the priest or deacon for all the faithful and kings and clergy, and afterwards the priestly doxology is added: "For you are merciful and by nature forgiving," for he suffered to show mercy to all, and nobody has the right to mercy of himself, but only through the divine kindness. After this Litany the Small Litany is recited, then the doxology: "For it is yours to have mercy, ..." etc.

CHAPTER 56. THE THREE SMALL ANTIPHONS IN ASMATIC VESPERS

First are sung the three antiphons, called 'small' because they do not consist of entire psalms, but of four verses selected from each, plus "Glory be ..." and "Now and ever ..." — three as typifying and honoring the Holy Trinity.

The first of these is: "I loved the Lord because he hears ..." [Ps 114]. Then the Theotokos is invoked by saying: "Through the prayers of the Theotokos, O Savior save us." For she loved God more than all logical creatures, having him indwelling through her supreme purity, and was designated worthy to reconcile us to our God and Father by incarnating the beloved Son. After these verses have been sung by both choirs plus "Glory be ..." and "Now and ever ...," the lesser Litany and

the ending of the priest's prayer: "By your grace and goodness . . ." for the only-begotten Son deigned to descend to us.

The second antiphon is: "I believed and therefore will I
speak . . ." [Ps 115] , and then the incarnate Lord is invoked by
saying: "Save us, O Son of God, who arose from the dead,
who sing to you . . .," or a verse for the feast, or " . . . who are
marvelous in your saints . . ." If it is the commemoration of a
saint rather than a Sunday or feast, "I believed and therefore
will I speak" shows the faith of the apostles and saints which
they drew all the nations from unbelief to belief, and "I will
receive the cup of salvation and call upon the name of the
Lord" [v. 4] indicates communion with Christ and salvation
through the blood. Through this the redeemed saints save us,
having communicated with Christ by witness and struggle,
and through them we are united with Christ. Therefore, after
"Glory be . . ." we say "O only-begotten Son . . ," indicating
his communion with us. This is expounded by the godly Cyril.
After "Now and ever . . ." we commemorate the most glorious
Mother of God, since through her the Only-begotten is united
with us. She is more excellent than all the holy angels and
mortals, and is their sanctification. After these verses with
"Glory be . . ." and "Now and ever . . ." again the Lesser
Litany and the ending of the priest's prayer: "For you are
holy, our God . . ."

Then the cantor begins the third antiphon, which is:
"Praise the Lord, all you nations . . ." [Ps 116] , calling all
the world to the angelic hymnody in honor of the Holy
Trinity. When these verses have been sung by both choirs
plus, "Glory be . . . " and "Now and ever . . . ," we add
"Holy God . . . , " "The Trisagion is sung loudly, while all
stand with heads uncovered, since they are praising God.

Behold in these three antiphons the harmony of the hymns
of the Church; for in the first antiphon the intercession of
the Mother of God is invoked, the second requests him who
became incarnate of her to show mercy through the mediation
of the saints, and the third and last one praises the thrice-holy
God with the angels, beseeching mercy—rising thus by degrees
to the highest things.

At the conclusion of this, the bishop signs thrice from his

throne or seat, typifying the Lord blessing from heaven. Then the Great Litany, the Petitions "Let us complete our prayer ..." by the deacon, "Peace be ..." and the Prayer of Head-bowing by the priest. This latter signifies our servanthood and humility towards God, and God's humbling himself even to the form of a servant. Then the priest raises his head and loudly and fervently recites the ending, indicating our resurrection from the body and death, and thanking our Savior: "May the power of your kingdom ..." Then the Lite is performed behind the ambon to propitiate God on behalf of all the faithful. We sing the resurrection verses of the Apostichon and "Glory be ..." and "Now and ever ..." Then the intercession is made by the priest, "Lord, have mercy" as is cutomary, as though before the tomb of Christ, and after "Hear us ..." the Apolytikia (Dismissal Hymns) and the Dismissal. If it is an ordinary day there is no Lite. The Apolytikion is sung while the priest is proceeding behind the ambon as a type of the Lite, singing "O Virgin Theotokos ..." After the priest intones "Let us beseech the Lord ... ," and "For you are our illumination Christ our God, and to you we ascribe glory ... ," i.e., you have given us light — both physical and intellectual — and you make the sun rise and set; and you are the true light which shines upon us, and after you have been taken up will come again to illuminate us. Thus, the Dismissal is performed. The final prayer of all is that of the head bowing and dismissal, similary at Matins and every other service also.

From what has been said, it is clear that the Asmatic Ser- with the saints of old are revelaed. Similarly, also in the hymns: the other takes its origin. Behold the order: for after the prayers it has us with heads bowed to show our servanthood, and thus it leads to the end of the prayers. It is most necessary to humble ourselves and to worship the Master, and to confess our servanthood.

If a feast occurs, or the commemoration of a saint, the appropriate lections are read after the conclusion of the Head-bowing, since through them the details of the feast hidden with the saints of old are revealed. Similarly also in the hymns; firstly, the psalms of David and of the other holy prophets are recited, since they anticipated it; then the hymns of grace are sung with them. Then, after the completion of all the hymns, the Martyrdoms of the feasts being celebrated are read.

This is how Vespers is performed, and Matins is spiritually similar to it also. Understand how marvelous everything is from the beginning of the creation; the Law and the Prophets typify and describe the details of the dispensation of the Savior, and in hymns and deeds we hand down and teach the things relating to our salvation, since through our Savior we have found the door and path to heaven.

CHAPTER 57. ASMATIC MATINS

I will explain the Matins of Sunday, of which the daily Matins is a copy, and then its order will be clear.

The royal doors of the church are closed, as typifying paradise and heaven of old— or rather, it is indeed paradise and heaven; paradise because in the midst of the church on the holy altar the tree of life (his most-holy cross) holds Christ performing his priestly office; heaven because the holy table is itself a throne, with Christ the king of glory seated there through the sacraments and the Gospels, and the angelic hosts round about, with the priestly orders, the Holy Chrism and sacred relics of the saints, the company of the souls of apostles and prophets departed and gone, yet still present through their holy writings, and the angels truly dwelling there as their concelebrants with us, and through the same hymn being sung by them and by us, performing the same Liturgy above and below. The doors of this holy temple of the new paradise and heaven are then closed. Because we close paradise and heaven to ourselves — and keep closing them — through our transgressions, the priest stands before the doors as a mediator, having the character of an angel, and blesses the one God in Trinity, saying: "Blessed be the kingdom of the Father and of the Son and of the Holy Spirit."

Then the Litany of Peace is recited, and "Pity, save . . . ," and the cantor chants part of the psalm to be sung in divine words: "And I awoke: Glory to you, O God." The priest continues: "Remembering our most holy . . . Lady . . . ," commending all to God, and praises him in the ending of the prayer: "For to you belongs all glory. . . " Then the cantor chants melodically: "I slept and I awoke: Glory to you, O God," thus beginning the psalm "Lord, how are they multiplied . . ." [Ps 3], with the rest of the psalms recited by verses, each choir saying : "Glory to you, O God." Three psalms are said together as typifying and glorifying the Trinity: "Lord, how are they multiplied . . ." [Ps 3], "O God, my God . . ." [Ps 62], and "Behold, bless the Lord . . ." [Ps 133]. On feast days triadic verses are sung to these also, i.e., "Glory to you, Father; glory to you, Son; glory to you, Holy Spirit, etc." On ordinary days and Sundays (except those of the Forefathers and the Fathers) only "Glory to you, O God" is sung; then "Glory be . . . ," and again "Glory to you, O God"; "Now and ever . . ." and the same versicle more loudly.

Then the priest sings: "Again and again . . . , " "Pity, save . . . "; and the cantor chants: "The inhabited world, Alleluia"; the priest: "Remembering our most-holy Lady . . ." and the ending of his prayer.

The cantor chants: "Blameless in the way, Alleluia. Blessed are those who are blameless in the way . . ." [Ps 118] with the rest of the verse and Alleluia. Then these verses are sung by both choirs with Alleluia, the whole first stasis (section) being completed. The "Glory be . . ." and "Now and ever . . . ," and again Alleluia. After that the priest recites the Lesser Litany; the cantor "Give me understanding, O Lord"; the priest: "Remembering our most-holy Lady . . ." and the ending of his prayer. Then the cantor sings: "Your hands have made me and fashioned me . . ." [v. 73] and the rest of the verse with the Hypopsalma (refrain), "Give me understanding, O Lord"; "Glory be . . ." and "Now and ever . . ." with the versicle "Give me understanding, O Lord" again. Then the priest intones the Lesser Litany, and the cantor: "The inhabited world, Alleluia"; the priest, Remembering our most-holy Lady . . ." and the ending of his prayer. The cantor sings: "Look upon me and have mercy upon me, Alleluia" [v. 132]. Then one of the doors of the temple is opened to show that heaven has been opened to us by the incarnation of the Lord, who looked down on us from heaven and became man through the heavenly and living gate, the Theotokos. Also before his passion and resurrection

he opened the heavens to us, as was written of his baptism—
that he saw the heavens split open—to us who were formerly
excluded. When he later ascended, he lead us up there.
These verses are recited by both choirs as far as "Let my
petition come before you, O Lord"[v.170]. Then as the dispensation is already completed—the Lord having suffered and
been offered through the sacrifice of the Cross, and we all
saved, both those in Hades and those on earth, through his resurrection, and enter heaven through his ascension — the doors
are opened by the priest. The entrance hymn is said in a loud
voice, with the Alleluia, and all enter as into heaven—the priest
going first and holding the cross, typifying the Lord who has
saved us through his cross. On the cross are fixed three candles,
signifying the light, since through the cross also the knowledge and glory of the Holy Trinity were revealed and shone
forth. After making the entrance the priest bows his head,
giving thanks to the Master. If a bishop is present, he also
bows his head with the priest and they recite the Prayer of
Entrance. The bishop makes the sign of the cross, saying:
"Blessed be the entrance of the saints, O Lord . . . , " and enters
the great doorway alone, preceded by the priests and deacon
as a type of the divine angels, typifying Christ (as already
stated) who opened to us the gates of paradise and heaven.
Entering, he praises and thanks him who opened the celestial
regions to us through the cross; our only leader, King and
God, who alone entered the world through the eastward-facing
gate [Ez 8.5], his ever-virgin Mother, and through her re-
opened to us the entrance to heaven. The others enter from
the sides or behind, since thus all following him we enter
heaven. The remainder of the psalm is sung by both choirs
standing in the middle of the church, expounding the resurrection of Christ and our life and salvation. "Let your hand
be moved to save me . . ." [v. 173]. Then "Glory be . . ." and
"Now and ever . .," and Alleluia is sung louder as a doxology
to him who rose again and raised us with him.

Then "All you works of the Lord, bless the Lord: praise
him and magnify him forever"[Canticle 8] melodically. While
this is being sung the entry is made, with the priest holding
the cross like an angel and the bishop typifying the Lord. The

bishop goes up to his throne, symbolizing the ascension and session of the Savior. (I call his seat "throne.") The cross is planted on the ambon opposite the altar, witnessing to the death and resurrection of the Savior and the confession of the Trinity through the three lighted candles on it. Then is sung the whole of the Canticle of the Three Youths, "Bless . . ." melodically and loudly—since they also typified the Holy Trinity in the furnace, glorifying the incarnation of the Word. Then: "Let us bless Father, Son and Holy Spirit, the Lord, now and forever"; and finally: "We praise, bless, hymn, and worship the Lord" again. Since through the One God the divine plan of the Holy Trinity and the Word (one person of the Trinity) all this grace has come to us, and we have been recalled from our great fall and raised up and illumined by the true light and led up into heaven, we, therefore, praise the Mother of God as the agent of the incarnation of the Word, saying: "You, the impregnable bastion, the fortress of salvation . . ."

CHAPTER 58. THE PRAYERS RECITED IN THE NARTHEX, THE CENSING THERE AND THE ENTRY: WHAT THESE THINGS SIGNIFY

It should be noted that during the first three psalms the priest offers the Matins Prayers to God. Then, when the "Blameless" [Ps 118] is begun, he takes the censer, puts on incense, and makes the sign of the cross. If there is a bishop present, he blesses the incense. The priest begins from the right side of the narthex—where the holy icon of the archangel is on the wall—and censes round the narthex the foundations of the church and the walls (those standing by the walls move out and back) returning to where he began. He makes the sign of the cross with the censer, saying: "Wisdom, be upstanding." He is preceded by one light only on feast days, with a few small lamps lighted in the narthex. When the cantor invites him, he intones: "Blessed are you, Lord . . ." — this being the customary verse at the end of the censing. The priest says in a low voice: "Wisdom, be upstanding," and proceeds to cense the bishop and subsequently everybody else. Then, entering the church from the side, he censes all the church in silence (it being closed, as stated above, and coming to the sanctuary he censes there and deposits the censer. Taking the sacred cross he stands behind the holy altar, not preceded by anyone nor by lights, but by the deacon only. Coming out from the other side he bows his head to the bishop and stands holding the cross in his right hand near the great doors of the church. There he remains until the end of the psalms. Then, after the three candles on the cross have been lit and the doors have been opened, the entrance takes place solemnly. This is not done without reason, but because of the marvelous and lofty significance of the sacred matters expounded, everything being well typified in divine knowledge and contemplation.

For this reason, we will examine it in more detail, repeating it again. The standing and chanting ouside the nave indicates our expulsion from paradise, as we stated above, and that heaven is closed to us, and that all the departed and the righteous are in the power of Hades. Therefore we stand at the west of the church, as being the darkness of hell and corruption, and as being subject to the horror of ignorance. We do not light big lamps because there is only partial light in us, the natural light of the knowledge of the just, of the prophets and of the Law, which is not able to enlighten totally. For the great and unsetting light, the sun of righteousness, has not yet shone upon us, nor has the grace of God been lightened upon us except to a small extent, obscurely and shadowily as typified by the censing taking place in the narthex, signifying the shadowy worship of the Law — which at that time encompassed only the nation of the Jews, a small one compared with all the other nations.

The censing is done initially around the walls and foundations, because the Church is built on the foundation of the apostles and prophets, beginnig with the Law of Moses and finishing with the truth and grace given through Christ. This is to signify that as the Tabernacle was built by Moses and Bezaleel in the Holy Spirit, so much more was the Church of Christ built and founded by divine grace—typifying his most holy body, formed in the Virgin from her pure and godly blood through the power of the Holy Spirit. Therefore, those standing around the walls of the church move away from them when the priest censes the foundations and then resume their places, signifying; first, that the Lord was conceived by the Virgin and made man; and secondly, that after we distance ourselves from him by sin we are re-united with him through his dispensation and re-sanctified by divine grace. This indicates first that we and the Church are hallowed by him, as happened also with the Tabernacle and the ancient Temple as a type of the Lord.

Then the priest enters the nave and censes it, thus honoring God in imitation of the ancient censing offered in the Holy of Holies—although more honorable than that priest, as enriched by the grace of the one great high-priest after the order of Melchisedek, our Savior Christ, and as an angel of almighty God also, as it is said: the priest propitiates God by the incense, and the people by their psalms, which thank and propitiate God, beseeching him to come and reveal himself to us. They also foreshadow the blameless life and behavior of our Savior, especially the one called "Blameless" [Ps 118], and also the lives of his saints and the passion and resurrection of the Savior. For this reason this psalm is sung particularly on Sundays and commemorations of saints, with the first, second, and third: "Blessed is the man." The only man blameless in the way is the Savior, and through his grace the saints are blameless also.

When the priest enters with the incense, then, as into the Holy of Holies, or rather into something loftier and holier than that, as commemorating and imitating the incense of Zachariah, who while censing in the sanctuary received the gift of John the preacher of grace, who was a forerunner in the preaching, baptism, life, and passion of our God. When (as I say) the priest enters, he takes the cross and comes forth in silence without candle-bearers, since Jesus our God came to us in humility and simplicity having fulfilled the Law. His cross was prefigured by the sufferings and preaching of the prophets, and he left us an example in his crucified life; having lived in holiness, he revealed to us the life with the cross which approaches the heavenly gate and angelic way of life. Having fulfilled all that the prophets had preached, he was crucified, died, and rose again, and sent his disciples to preach and baptize in the name of the Father and of the Son and of the Holy Spirit. For this reason, we light three candles on the revered cross, since after the curcifixion he rose again and appeared to us with the marks of the nails and ascended into heaven, and took us up also. This is the signification of the cross which the priest holds when he enters with the bishop. Then everybody enters together, since Christ renewed and prepared for us a short way through the veil of the flesh, and by this means we have the entrance to the sanctuary, where the great high-priest entered before, effecting our eternal redemption and salvation in the life to come.

Thus we all enter together with him and bear his reproach, i.e., the cross on which he suffered for us outside Jerusalem. This is why the cross is carried outside the nave, so that we can enter with him into heaven, who is king of heaven, and enter paradise through our Savior since he already suffered outside Jerusalem for mankind, who was tempted inside Eden and conquered by the serpent, delivered over to death, and finally expelled from Paradise.

These are the matters relating to Matins. A reading has been set from the Synaxarion, since it refers to those who suffered for Christ and died in holiness for him, imitating and emulating him—otherwise it refers to the current feast. Then the Litany is recited again, and "Have mercy upon me, O God" [Ps 50] with the appropriate refrain, which we call "pentecostarion."

CHAPTER 59. THE 50TH PSALM

It is called "pentecostarion" because the psalm is the 50th. This relates to David's crimes of murder and adultery, and is appropriate for all pious mortals, since it is a psalm of repentance, since the first of the race of Adam killed himself and all mankind, and comitted adultery by eating of the tree forbidden to him. Through this he lost the God-likeness which he did not possess by nature, since he was not God, but a creature. Thus, this psalm is relevant and appropriate for all sinful humans. This is why it is sung in church particularly to invoke the mercy of God and seek forgiveness of sins and purity of heart, and for the Holy Spirit to be renewed in us and not leave us, whom we lost by contaminating ourselves with unlimited sins; and for the offering of a contrite heart as a sacrifice to God, i.e., repentance instead of the ancient sacrifice of animals.

At this point it prefigures the message of the Gospel and abolishes the things of the Law as shadowy and imperfect. For it is not possible for a logical being to be saved by an offering of mindless animals unless he corrects himself by means of his soul. He is corrected if he repents fully and offers in his place a sinless man, that is, Jeus Christ the Son of God, who for our sake became man and gave himself as an appropriate sacrifice for all. Moreover, the psalm reveals the hope that the New Jerusalem, i.e., the Church, will be built when she prophesies that a sacrifice of praise, i.e., the confession of Christ will be offered, and the fatted calf which is the Lord himself.

The Pentecostarion is recited verse by verse by the two choirs, with the Apolytikion of the day/feast/saint as appropriate. On feasts of our Lord "Glory be . . . " and "Now and ever . . ." of the feast is said; on ordinary days, that of the day is said, and to "Cast me not away from your presence" is said "Only-begotten Son"; and to "Now and ever" is said "The most glorious."

Then, immediately the Kanons of the feast or saint are sung, which we have added for the adornment and harmony of the church, and for the glory of God and his saints. We add verses up to eight if there are two Kanons, to six if there is a commemoration of a major saint, or four if no saint is commemorated. We have added these also for the profit, consolation, and perseverance of the pious, since they are used to these in the Kanons. Formerly Kanons were not sung in Asmatic Matins; but after Psalm 50 and the petitions, the Psalms (Lauds) were recited immediatly. However, now the Exaposteilaria are said after the Kanons, then the petitions, and immediately "Praise the Lord" [Ps 148.1] . The cantor of the first choir sings: "Praise the Lord from the heavens: to you praise is due, O God," and the other choir sings the same to the next verse, and the other six verses are recited similarly.

From this, it is clear that the Monastic Psalms have their origin in the Asmatic one, since they also recite it similarly at the start: "To you praise is due, O God." To "Praise the Lord from the earth" they say: "Give glory to God," and similarly to the remaining six verses; to "His name is exalted" they add: "To him praise is due," etc., to "Let them praise his name" they say: "Glory to you, Holy Father," and similarly to the other verse; to "The praises of God"—"Son of God, have mercy upon us," and to the other verse; and to "To bind their kings in chains"—"Speak to us, Lord, through the Holy Spirit." For the Lord is Spirit, as Paul says [2 Cor 3.17] that the Trinity might be praised. Similarly the remaining verses: to "Praise God in his saints" they say: "Son of God, have mercy upon us," and the following ones similarly, because of the incarnation. To "Praise him on the well-tuned cymbals" and the following verse they add: "Glory to you who have revealed the light." Then "Blessed be the Lord God of Israel" [Canticle 9]. This they say to all the verses, since this canticle is a prophecy of the incarnation of the Word of God, and a prelude to it and a thanksgiving. It was uttered near to the birth of the Baptist and Forerunner, and the church sings it solemnly every day as a thanksgiving canticle. To "Glory be" is said in a louder voice: "Blessed be the Lord and King Jesus, for he visited . . ." and so on; similarly to "Now and ever" — "Glory be to you, O God," melodically in full. The, "Let us all hymn the Mother of God, through whom we receive forgiveness of sins and health for our souls." These verses exalt the prophesied dispensation of Christ, especially through the birth of the Baptist, as we said above.

Then "Glory be to God on high" is said from the ambon by a reader who takes the cross in his hands and stands on the ambon, and the Great Doxology is added by the cantors. This is recited daily, and on Sunday the Psalms are recited in the mode, with the refrains and Resurrection Stichera; and finally either the Stichera of the feast or the saint, if there is a commemoration, "Glory be, " and the Eothinon.

Then the entrance of the priest with the holy gospel takes place, symbolizing the resurrection of the Savior which occurred at dawn. This is why the priests bow their heads during the Eothinon and recite the Prayer of Entry, as a type of the humility and condescension of the Lord who descended to us and to Hades; and when they have lifted their heads as a sign of the resurrection, they raise the gospel— this also proclaims the resurrection—and "Wisdom, be upstanding" is said as a proclamation of the resurrection.

After this, to "Now and ever" is sung "Most blessed are you, O Theotokos," since through her our salvation was granted and the curse of Eve lifted. When the priests have entered, the cantor holding the cross on the ambon says "Glory be to God on high," and then it is sung asmatically by the cantors. Meanwhile, within the holy sanctuary, it is recited in full by the priests, so that the doxology is in harmony outside also, since we were made one church, in heaven and on earth. through Christ, to the proclamation and glorification of the holy resurrection of our Savior Christ.

For this reason, also, we sing to a sweet melody three times, on one Sunday "Today salvation"; on the next "Arissen from the tomb . . . — both outside by the cantors and inside by the priests. This arrangement represents clearly to us the resurrection of the Savior. Thus "Arise O Lord" [Ps 131.8] is sung immediately, followed by the Matins Gospel sung by a priest from the ambon, since he manifests the more perfect order of angels. After this the Litany is said, the Great Petitions, the Head bowing, and the Dismissal.

This, then, is how Matins is performed. We have described the matters relating to the full Liturgy above.

CHAPTER 60. TRITHEKTE DURING THE FASTS, AND THE LITURGY OF THE PRESANCTIFIED

Now we will speak of Trithekte during the fasts, which it is necessary to join with the Liturgy performed during Holy Lent in catholic churches by secular priests, which preserves

the type of the great catholic Holy Liturgy as far as the Great
Entrance. This was devised by the ancient Fathers so that a
complete Liturgy would be not performed during Holy Lent.
This is how Trithekte is performed. Receiving the signal to
begin, the deacon says, "Bless, master!"— the priest, "Blessed
be the Kingdom . . ." — the deacon: the Litany of Peace. The
priest reads the prayer of the First Antiphon, "O God who
sittest upon the cherubim . . ." and sings aloud the ending:
"For you are our God, the God of pity . . ."; then the cantors
read the whole of the psalm "To you, Lord, have I lifed my
soul" [Ps 24] in the mode; "Through the prayers of the
Theotokos . . ."; "Glory be . . . ," "Now and ever . . ." in the
same mode. Then the deacon says: "Again and again," while
the priests reads secretly the prayer of the second Antiphon:
"We bessech you, Lord God . . ." with the ending aloud: "For
glorified is your all-holy name . . ." Then the cantors sing as the
second antiphon the whole psalm "The Lord is my light and my
salvation. . ." [Ps 26] and the versicle: "Save us, Son of God,
who sing to you Alleluia," "Glory be . . . ," "Now and ever . . ."
in the same mode. Once more the deacon says "Again and
again" while the priest recites secretly the third prayer: "Lord
God Almighty . . ." with the ending aloud: "For you are gracious . . ." The third antiphon is sung with a double Alleluia. At
the verse "Walking in the path of righteousness . . ." [Ps 100.6]
as in one verse until the end of the psalm, the entrance of the
priest and deacon takes place from the sanctuary to the choir
—without candles and incense, as symbolizing the leading
away of the Lord to the Cross, which took place at the sixth
hour. This is why it is performed at the Trithekte. The
deacon says: "Bless, master, the holy entry," and the priest
recites the prayer: "Blessed be the entry of your saints, Lord,
always, now and forever." As state, this entry symbolizes
the dragging away of the Savior to the cross, since he was
taken away and crucified at the sixth hour, when the thief
crucified with him found paradise in a few words of repentance. For this reason, the deacon and priest are vested in
purple, signifying by this the passion and death of the Lord.
After the Entrance, the deacon again recites the Litany of
Peace, while the priest reads the prayer: "O Lord God of our

fathers . . . ," the prayer of the Sixth Hour, praying for us to be protected "from the arrow that flies by day, the pestilence that walks in darkness, the attack of the demon of noonday" [Ps 90.5-6], and entreating God for other things. He sings aloud the ending: "For to you is due . . . ," and then the cantors sing the Troparion of the Prophecy, and the lector on the ambon reads the prophecy. After that the deacon says: "Let us all say . . . ," while the priest recites secretly the prayer of the Litany of intercession, with the ending aloud: "For you are merciful . . ." And the remainder is done according to the pattern of the Liturgy after the Gospel. The reading from Isaiah is read as a type of the Epistle plus Gospel, since he preaches concerning the Savior more clearly than the others, and particularly concerning his passion. It is clear that this is an ancient custom from the Fathers, since in the monasteries also the Prophecy of Isaiah is read at the Sixth Hour throughout the whole of Lent, and that of Ezekiel during Holy Week as foretelling the passion and resurrection of the Savior. Then the deacon says: "Pray, catechumens . . ." and the priest reads the Prayer for the Cathechumens. From Mid-lent Wednesday the deacon recites the petitions for those preparing for Holy Baptism and the priest reads the prayer for them: "O Lord our God, make known your mercies . . . ," with the ending aloud: "For you are our illumination . . ." The deacon again says the usual "All catechumens . . . ," while the priest reads the First Prayer for the Faithful: "O Lord our God, who has saved us from polytheistic error . . ." The deacon says: "Wisdom arise! " and the priest: "For you are our God . . ." Then the deacon recites the Litany of Peace, while the priest reads the Second Prayer for the Faithful: "O Lord our God, who is a short time . . ."; the deacon: "Wisdom!"; the priest: "For blessed and glorified . . ."; the deacon: "Let us complete our prayer to the Lord . . . ," etc. The priest says the great prayer: "O Lord our God, the only good and gracious . . . ," in which also the crucifixion of the Savior is commemorated, and his resurrection and ascension. He prays also for the grace of God to come upon us, and strengthen and enlighten us, etc., and entreats God for what is necessary and profitable; and finally that the grace and mercy of God may be with us always; and sings the ending aloud: "For yours is the power . . ." Then: "Peace be to all"; the deacon: "Let us bow our heads . . . ," while the priest reads the Prayer of Head bowing: "O Lord our God, who sits on the throne of glory . . . " with the ending aloud: "May the all-holy name of your graciousness be blessed and glorified . . . "; the deacon: "Let us go forth in peace," and when the priest has come out of the sanctuary they proceed together behind the ambon, that in the midst of all they may glorify God, and begin Vespers.

[Vespers]

The deacon says: "Let us beseech the Lord," and the priest facing east intones: "Blessed be the glory of the Lord from his holy place, always, now and ever and to ages of ages." During processional litanies, this is the beginning of the litany, being said by the bishop behind the ambon; hence it is the start of Vespers. Then, at the side of the church, Vespers is sung by the cantors as an intercession. There the Psalter is read, and the verses of the Triodion and Menaion according to the pattern of the monasteries, and "Gladdening light . . ." and "Deign . . . ," since it is a monastic and penitential service; and the idiomelon of the aposticon, "Now lettest," "Trisagion," "O Virgin Theotokos . . ." "Lord, have mercy" is not said, nor are prostrations made, nor the dismissal, nor are lamps lit until the Lection from Proverbs in the Presanctified. After "O Virgin Theotokos . . . " and the rest as usual, all go to their places.

CHAPTER 61: WHY THE PROCESSIONAL LITANIES TAKE PLACE OUTSIDE, AND THE CROSSES AND HOLY ICONS ARE CARRIED AROUND DURING THEM

It should be known that the (processional) litanies take place outside — either in the narthex or around the monasteries or cities — to remind us of our expulsion, that we have been set outside Eden to humble ourselves and realize that

we are unworthy of the holy places, expelees from paradise
and heaven. We should copy the Publican who stood far off
out of great reverence, and the Prodigal Son who departed to a
foreign land. On the crossroads and roads we make petitions
so that these, which have been tainted by our sins, may be
purified. And, taking the holy icons from the churches, we
carry them around, and the sacred crosses and relics of the
saints often also, so that the dwellings and roads, the waters
and air, the earth polluted by our treading it, and inhabited
town and country, may be sanctified together with the
people and share in the divine grace, rejecting what pollutes
and destroys so that he may be merciful to us, who became
incarnate for us and assumed the form of a servant, which is
born and pictured by the holy icons and the figures of his
saints who dwelt in purity on earth; and that he who trod
this earth for our sake, God incarnate, and was crucified for
us, might save us who confess this work of extreme goodness
and love, his shedding his blood through the cross and dying
for us; and through possessing and showing these tokens of
his passion, the sacred images of the cross, by which he who
suffered death on the cross for us conquered the enemy and
saved us from death.

[Vespers and Presanctified]

When the deacon receives the signal, he says: "Bless,
Master!"; and the priest: "Blessed be the kingdom of the
Father . . ." Then the deacon recites the Litany of Peace;
the Asmatic Vespers is sung from "Incline, O Lord . . ." [Ps
85] after the ending sung aloud, to the end. During this the
priest reads the prayers of Vespers. Then the completion of the
day, "Lord, I have cried . . ."[Ps 140], the verses as usual,
and the Entrance of the priest and deacon— or of the priest
only — without candles, his remaining first is silence indicating our sitting in darkness. And at: "For to you, Lord . . ."
[Ps 140.9], the cantor calls him, and he enters the sanctuary.
The verses are completed with the Hypopsalma [refrain], to
"With my voice I called to the Lord" [Ps 141]. Then: Glory

. . .'' and ''Now and ever . . . ,'' and hypopsalma in full. Then all sit and the lection from Genesis is read from the ambon. While this is being read, two portable candlesticks — or more if a bishop is present — and the censer are prepared in the sanctuary. If a deacon is serving with the priest, only the deacon comes out holding the censer and candle together, preceded by the lectors with the candlesticks. If there is no deacon, the priest comes out alone holding the candle and censer, preceded by the lectors, and passes down the side to the back of the the church.

CHAPTER 62. WHY THERE ARE LIGHTS AT THE PROVERBS LECTION AT VESPERS, AND THE SIGNIFICANCE OF ''THE LIGHT OF CHRIST SHINES UPON ALL.''

When the Genesis reading is finished, the deacon or priest appears immediately with the lights, the Royal Doors being open and all standing. In the middle of the church he makes the sign of the cross with the censer intoning: ''Wisdom, arise! The light of Christ shines upon all,'' then goes up to the sanctuary. Then the lector on the ambon reads the lection from Proverbs, and the usual lights in the church are lit. This signifies that at the end of the age the true light, Jesus Christ in flesh, has shone upon us who sit in darkness and filled the world with the grace of his light. This is why at the end of Vespers we say: ''For thou art our illumination, O Christ our God . . .'' This takes place after the reading from Genesis, when Proverbs is begun; for Genesis recounts the beginning, the Creation and the Fall of Adam, while Proverbs teaches about the Son of God, exhorting those who have been adopted by him as sons. It calls the same son Wisdom, saying she [Wisdom] has built a house for herself — his most holy body — in which there are seven pillars — all the gifts of the Spirit — and through the proper bread of his body and the cup of his blood he gives us to eat and drink, and is the light illuminating what is in heaven and on earth. For in wisdom God established the earth; it is said that he prepared the heavens in prudence, as David also says: "In wisdom have you made them all" [Ps 103.24]. It is clear that this light signifies the true light of Jesus Christ. For the deacon serving with the priest approaches him or the presiding bishop with the lighted candle before going out, saying: "Bless the light, Master"; and the bishop or priest blesses the light, saying: "For you are our illumination, O Christ our God, always . . . " And thus the deacon comes out before the reading from Proverbs. After Proverbs is sung immediately: "Let my prayer arise . . . " [Ps 40.2 etc.] and then the rest of the service of the Presanctified as usual.

CHAPTER 63. WE MUST PROSTRATE OURSELVES COMPLETELY AT THE ENTRANCE OF THE PRESANCTIFIED

At the entrance with the gifts we must prostrate ourselves completely, since the Holy Gifts are consecrated and truly our Savior himself. For this is what is contained in the —his most holy body with the divine blood. At the end of the Liturgy, the Prayer behind the Ambon is recited, being propitiatory, dismissive, and petitionary, that we may see the resurrection and celebrate it here also; behind the ambon in the center of the church, to be heard and prayed by all, as before God for all the people. And when the Liturgy is finished the Pannychis begins. Behold now the order of the Pannychis also.

CHAPTER 64. THE PANNYCHIS DURING THE FIRST WEEK OF HOLY LENT

During the first week, after the Prayer behind the Ambon, the priest (or the bishop, if one is present) blesses the cantor. Then the cantor chants: "He who dwells in the secret place of the Most High" [Ps 90]. The priest, meanwhile, reads the prayer in the sacristy while arranging the holy vessels. After "Glory be" and "Now and ever," the petitions are made and he sings aloud "To you belongs glory . . . "

The cantor then sings the First Antiphon "I cried to the Lord in my oppression" [Ps 119] with the refrain "As merci-

ful, O Lord." The verses are sung together with this by each
choir, according to the season. Meanwhile, the priest reads
the Prayer of the First Antiphon. After "Glory be" and
"Now and ever" the full refrain, then the priest recites the
Lesser Litany and sings aloud "For hallowed and glorified."
Then the left-hand choir begins the Second Antiphon "To
you, Lord, I have lifted my soul" [Ps 24], with the refrain
"The gate of your mercy." While the verses are being sung
with this, the priest reads the Prayer of the Second, "You
the unfading and unsetting light," joining on the other two
two prayers "Unsleeping and ceaseless praise" and "Lord
almighty and incomprehensible." There are some wonderful
prayers, especially those of the Pannychis. After "Glory be"
and "Now and ever" and the full refrain, the priest reads the
Lesser Litany and sings aloud "For you are gracious . . ."
The Third Antiphon is sung, "I rejoiced when they said to me"
[Ps 121] with "Have mercy upon us, O Lord, have mercy
upon us," while the priest, holding a lighted candle and the
censer, censes first the sanctuary, then the nave, and the con-
gregation according to ancient custom. If there is a deacon,
he holds the candle and precedes the priest. After "Glory be"
and "Now and ever," the refrain is not said in full, but only
the end of the troparion, "O Lord, have mercy upon us."

Then immediately the cantor adds the 50th Psalm "Have
mercy upon me, O God," adding by verses "Merciful Lord,
have mercy upon us." The whole psalm is sung by each choir,
"Glory be," "Now and ever," and the full refrain. Consider
the psalms sung and the troparia with them, and you will find
a triple text, for there are three antiphons and three troparia,
in honor of the Trinity and relating to it. Therefore, it is full
of humility, confession, and penitence. Again, the last psalm,
the 50th, with "Lord, have mercy" in penitence calls upon
the Lord for mercy.

Then the deacon sings "Let us entreat the Lord," and the
priest "For you are holy . . . " "Let all that breathes . . ." is
sung, and the first of the priests reads the Gospel from the
ambon. Then immediately is sung "The incorporeal nature,"
compiled of verses. It theologizes on the Trinity, and calls
upon all the choirs of the saints to intercede. Then the cantor

adds aloud thrice "Lord, have mercy," and everyone continues it 100 times. The priest reads secretly the Prayer of
Head bowing "O Lord our God, incline our hearts." At the
conclusion of the "Lord, have mercy," the deacon says
"Again let us entreat that we may be heard," three times
more the "Lord, have mercy," and the priest "Hear us . . ."
Do you see how wonderful this arrangement is, that through
the priest as intercessor praying within secretly, the petitions
of the people are brought before God?

Then "Blessed be the name of the Lord," since we come
to physical need, to nourishment, but not without sanctification, for we receive food previously blessed. While "I will bless
the Lord" is said, the distribution of the antidoron takes
place and the Dismissal.

This then is the Asmatic Service, most necessary and most
ancient, performed with a priest as a type of Jesus as intercessor
to God, as we have said repeatedly, and having the power to
intercede from ordination by the grace of God. This order
preserves the sevenfold praising also; the things performed in
the narthex belong to the Midnight Service, but those performed inside to Matins. The Trithekte fulfills the Third and
Sixth Hours together; the things of the Ninth typify the
Lamp-lighting, those of the Asmatic Vespers — Vespers itself,
and those of the Pannychis — Compline. However, now
through sloth has been lost what used to be kept by catholic
churches, whether always or at times, to preserve the ancient
tradition intact. In monasteries and other churches, the
service is sung the same, the monastic way. But we have expounded this to you who perform and keep it by the grace
of God; and in brief we considered the matters relating to
this to the glory of our Lord Jesus Christ.

CHAPTER 65. THE HOLY BREAD OF THE PANAGIA, WHICH IS ELEVATED

Since we have completed this discourse, we will mention
some small points concerning the holy bread of the Panagia
which is elevated, and finally we will expound the matters

relating to our end, so as to end our discourse with matters of our end.

The bread elevated with the invocation of our most-holy Lady was appointed to be raised at the end of the monastic meal, for the sanctification of the monks and as a seal on the food they have eaten— but also especially in honor of the Mother of God, who brought forth for us the heavenly bread which lives and continues forever nourishing our souls. It is also elevated for our assistance at any other time whenever somebody has need, and in the Holy Liturgy it is often elevated on behalf of supplicants, although customarily it is performed by many priests desiring to invoke and praise the all-praised One, particularly when the mysteries of her son and our God are offered, so that we may receive greater assistance through her. It is elevated in the Holy Liturgy where it is customary to commemorate her, e.g., at "Especially remembering our most-holy Lady . . . ," and in all our need and danger we invoke her as the most sure helper and protector. Through the elevation of this bread we obtain great assistance, as we have often seen in practice and learnt from many other reliable persons. For it is not merely the words said at the elevation of the bread, but the invocation and supplication of our one God in Trinity, and the invocation of our most-holy Theotokos and the request for assistance, including the mystery of our faith, the confession, the hope of our salvation. Therefore, at the monastic table, first, thanks is given (for how could this be blessed without word and order — the table of the servants of the Word of God being that of the only pure, holy, and living bread, who created and creates everything by His word, as the living Wisdom of the One God) and the "Our Father," the prayer for our daily bread. When this has been completed, the tripartite loaf is taken out on behalf of all, symbolizing the Trinity and its unity in every way: the Trinity by its corners and sections, the unity by the one raised center. Thus, if you turn this loaf, it has three corners and the center ends in a point. By apostolic tradition handed down orally by the Fathers from the beginning, by custom we daily offer this section of the loaf to the one God in Trinity in the name of the Theotokos. For she gave birth in the flesh to one person of the Trinity, since she is truly Theotokos and is hymned as such.   For she brought to us the living manna and is the mother of the divine chalice.

CHAPTER 66. ORDERLINESS AT THE DINING OF THE MONKS AND OTHER PRAYERS

When this bread has been placed in a holy vessel set apart for this and blessed by the priest, a candle is lit on it and the priest makes the sign of the cross over the food, calling upon our God Jesus Christ to bless it. During dining, holy discourses are read so that we may do all to the glory of God as we have been taught. "For whether you eat or drink, do all to the glory of God" [1 Cor 8.31] and "Sanctify all by the word of God and supplication" [1 Ti 4.5] it is said.   This is why the sign of the cross and the prayer takes place.   Holy discourses are read, lest like animals we should only consider our stomachs —but being logical beings with bodies, we strengthen the body by what is eaten and the soul by what is read. After eating, we all rise and say a prayer glorifying God; with David blessing Him who has mercy upon us and has nourished us from our youth. Then we say "Glory to you, Holy One glory to you, Lord, for giving us food to cheer us," and the rest which Chrysostom interprets concerning these things.

CHAPTER 67. THE ELEVATION OF THE BREAD OF OUR ALL-HOLY LADY (PANAGIA)

When all this has been performed with praise, he that has read and serves the brothers in spiritual matters comes forward, and having asked he receives forgiveness, since forgiveness cleanses and it is necessary to be pure in order to employ pure things. While all stand silently, he elevates the bread and chants: "Great is the name," and all reply: "Of the Holy Trinity."   Then making the sign of the cross he adds: "Most holy Theotokos, help us," and we all say together: "Through her intercessions, O God, have mercy upon us and save us.   You are confessed and hymned by us, Holy Trinity, save us. You are confessed and hymned by us, Holy Trinity, who alone are God. There is none beside you, our creator and sustainer," Then they add the hymn to the Mother of God, "All generations bless you . . . ," because of her prophecy, and at the end of this the angelic salutation, "Hail, most favored One, the Lord is with you," since this message was the start of our salvation, adding "And through you the Lord is with us," i.e., by grace. Then harmoniously and melodically with heads uncovered, to show that she is our head who gave birth to Christ, our protection from heaven, our provider and salvation, they sing: "Worthy it is . . . , "confessing her as Theotokos and more honored than the Cherubim, who received the Divine Word enhypostatized in her womb and bore him without corruption. Essentially and principally we magnify her as Theotokos, taking from her canticle "We magify you"; and then "We bless you" — for she said "My soul magnifies the Lord,'" and "For from henceforth all generations shall bless me."

The elevation is offered to God, since we say "Great is the name of the Holy Trinity," confessing the God of all in Trinity, for to him we offer the bread and magnify his name. In saying "Most holy Theotokos help us" we also confess the incarnation of the Word. For this is what the words of the Theotokos mean, and she is supplicated since we believe she is present and ready to assist. The bread is offered as a gift to her on our behalf, or rather through her to her Son, who became man through her and willingly suffered on the cross for us, which is why the elevation is done in the form of a cross.

This bread has great power then, having had the divine name invoked upon it, and first the sign of the cross and then that of the Theotokos, confessing the incarnation of the Word and invoking the assistance of the Mother of God. It saves us from many perils, fills us with all benefits, and saves us continually. This is why we should do this always by day and by night at every hour, performing all the prayers, magnifying the Trinity, and calling upon the Theotokos for assistance. For who is of greater assistance than she? Or who has greater access to God? Or who can save better than she? Since I regard this as one of the greatest things, I always recite all these divine words and encourage others to do this as often as possible. You know well that I have transmitted this to be done every day at Matins at the end of the Ninth Ode, for the priest to elevate this bread and say these customary holy phrases, as has been handed down to us by the fathers as a confession of the Holy Trinity (the only God of all, as we said) and of the incarnation of the divine Word, and in honor of his mother (the only ever-virgin Theotokos) to petition and request her help. Since we have received great assistance from this, I beseech you in Christ, and recommend and advise all of you not to neglect this for your common salvation. For if some of the heterodox recite "Hail most favored one" morning and evening, zealously saying this always and honoring the pure Theotokos (although this was not devised by them, but is an ancient patristic custom, as you will learn shortly), how much more ought we to do this zealously and unfailing, who are Orthodox and children of the true catholic Church.

That it was the custom earlier to chant "Hail most favored . . ." is apparent from the Vespers of Holy Lent, where above all else, after "Our Father," we say immediately "O Virgin Theotokos, hail most favored one, the Lord is with you . . ."; and after Vespers at Vigils, when this is always recited before the blessing of the loaves; and similarly in the Asmatic Service, it is customary always to recite this at Vespers, since this occurs as you see in this Great Church of the Thessalonians. So, if it is necessary to say "Hail, most favored one," since this tends to the honor and glory of the Mother of God and is the angelic salutation through which the curse for sin was lifted and joy was granted (i.e., the Savior of all, God the Divine Word, dwelt in her and became man through her), how much more necessary is it that this divine and patristic ceremony should be performed? For all the Typika and the ancient customs which have been transmitted to us from the fathers testify that this is a divine service the elevation of the bread — an offering to God and a confession of the Trinity, the invoking and petitioning of the holy Theotokos, which takes place for our assistance. It is good and acceptable also to sing to her "All generations bless you" as prophesied by her and handed down (as we said) and "We magnify you." One should also recite the angelic salutation "Hail, most favored one, the Lord is with you," for in her he became enhypostatically incarnate and now dwells by grace on our behalf, by whom as Isaiah says "God" became and is "with us" [Is 7.14]. For this reason we beseech her, crying: "Through you (God is) with us." May he always be so, through her. Amen.

Cleric: All this is very useful and necessary, Master, especially as it has been ordered and handed down to us to do, and we are zealous. We do this in the catholic churches, as you have commanded. May we perform the divine service untiringly always, through your holy prayers.

Hierarch: May God grant this to you and me through the intercessions of the Mother of God, since we all need the assistance of her prayers. It is necessary and useful to perform this continually and to invoke the saints as mediators, especially the most pure Mother of God, who is holy and able to save us above all others; for each of us is guilty of many faults. Let us now turn to our end and fulfill our promise.

INDEX

A

Aaron, 25, 71
Adam, 24, 63, 85, 93
Aeneas, 15
Amalek, 30
Antioch, 21, 71
Arios, Arians, 37
Asmatic Service, 3, 4, 5, 21, 71,
    72, 79, 86, 87, 92, 96, 100
Athanasios the Great, St., 23, 34
Athenogenes, martyr, 60

B

Balfour, David, 1
Basil, St., 36
Bezaleel, 83

C

Cathedral Rite, see Asmatic Service
Chariton, confessor, 22
Constantinople, 13, 25, 71
Cyril, St., 77

D

Daniel, 12, 49
David, 9, 18, 20, 23, 25, 27, 31,
    34, 35, 36, 38, 46, 47, 67,
    70, 74, 85, 94, 98
Demetrios, St., 1
Dialogue, 2f.
Diocletian, 30
Dionysios the Areopagite, 3, 4

E

Eden, 64, 85, 91
Eustathios, martyr, 25
Euthymios, 22
Ezekiel, 9, 12, 90

F

Flavianos, patriarch of Antioch,
    37

G

Gregory of Nyssa, St., 23

H

Habbakuk, 31
Hagia Sophia, Thessalonike, 3, 79
Hagia Sophia, Constantinople, 3
    21, 22
Hannah, 31
Holy Wisdom, see Hagia Sophia

I

Ignatios, 13, 14
Isaiah, 9, 12, 31, 34, 35, 90, 101

J

Jerusalem, 31, 70, 85, 86
Job, 40, 67
John St., 12, 16, 45
John the Baptist, St., 34, 61, 84,
    87
John Chrysostom, St., 13, 98
John Damascene, St., 22
John of the Ladder, St., 13
Jonah, 32
[Julian] the Apostate, 30

K

Kallistos, 13, 14

M

Mary St., 4, 5, 25, 26, 31, 32,
    33, 44, 45, 46, 48, 56, 57,
    58, 62, 65, 67, 68, 70, 72,
    75, 76, 78, 80, 81. 83, 84,

87, 91, 96, 97, 98, 99, 100, 101
Maximin, 30
Maximos the Confessor, 3
Melchisedek, 84
Meletios, patriarch of Antioch, 37
Miriam, 31
Moses, 12, 14, 25, 31, 44, 71, 83

N

Nikephoros, 13

O

Og, 30

P

Panagia, see Mary, St.
Paul, St., 12, 13, 14, 15, 23, 34, 53, 54, 67, 87
Peri ton hieron teleton kai theion mysterion tes Ekklesias, ix
Peter, St., 15, 40
Peter the Fuller, 36
Pharaoh, 30
Phountoules, Ioannes, 1, 6

S

Sabas, St., 22
Sabellios, 37

Samuel, 31
Sion, 30
Solomon, 71
Sophronios, patriarch, 22
Stephan, St., 14
Symeon of Thessalonike, St., canonization of, xi, 2; life of, 1-2; liturgical activity of, 2-6
Symeon the New Theologian, 13

T

Theodosios the Younger, 36
Theoktistos, 22
Theotokos, see Mary St.
Thessalonike, 21, 71
Three Youths, 32
Treatise on Prayer, 3

X

Xanthopouloi, Monastery of, 1

Z

Zachariah, 32, 84